Eleven Things That Art is NOT

by

Marcus Darc

Disclaimer:

The facts in this book are, to the best of my knowledge, true. I do not, however, consider my knowledge to be infallible, and therefore leave myself open to correction. The opinions, deliberations, speculations and conclusions are as true to me as I can get them at this moment in time. Should you decide to take on any of these ideas, realise that they do, at that point, become your own, and responsibility shall only be taken for the good things that come of it. No claim is made for any miracles, but you never know what might happen when you shake up a few core beliefs.

First edition published October 2019

Darc Productions in association with KDP Publishing

Cover artwork by Micky Betts (*Mixter Art*)

ISBN: 9781659413878

website: www.thedarcone.com

email: marcus@thedarcone.com

©2018 by Marcus Darc
All rights reserved

Contents

- Important first step — Pg.1
- Introduction — Pg.3
- Chapter 1 – the First *Not* — Pg.19
- Chapter 2 – the Second *Not* — Pg.35
- Chapter 3 – the Third *Not* — Pg.63
- Chapter 4 – the Fourth *Not* — Pg.75
- Chapter 5 – the Fifth *Not* — Pg.85
- Chapter 6 – the Sixth *Not* — Pg.91
- Chapter 7 – the Seventh *Not* — Pg.105
- Chapter 8 – the Eighth *Not* — Pg.111
- Chapter 9 – the Ninth *Not* — Pg.123
- Chapter 10 – the Tenth *Not* — Pg.137
- Chapter 11 – the Eleventh *Not* — Pg.157

- Summary   Pg.185
- References   Pg.197
- Bibliography   Pg.203

Important First Step

So that we have a reference point with which to align the information we are about to cover, I would like you to do something – right now. I want you to bring to mind an occasion when you were truly touched by a work of art. Everyone has one. It could have been a piece of music, a great painting or sculpture, the recital of a poem, a particularly moving scene in a play or film, a spellbinding piece of literature. We're after a time when a piece of art really moved you, reached you and went through you. Whatever form it took, take yourself there now; re-experience this moment. How did it make you feel? What state of mind was aroused? Close your eyes and contact this as closely as you are able.

Do you have it?

Good.

That you complete this exercise is imperative to understanding all that follows, so please do not skimp on this step. Go back and grasp it thoroughly. As you do, take note that this is not an everyday, run-of-the-mill experience. It doesn't equate with feeding the cat or catching the bus or coming home exhausted from work and collapsing on the sofa. This moment was out of the gulf-stream of the daily flow of life, in a separate passage of time where time has no significance. It gave you something. You might not be able to put what it was into words, but it gave you something nonetheless.

We shall refer to this experience throughout this book as your *Prime Experience*. There is no particular significance to the name, it being used merely for reference, but for now just make note that you have had such an experience and that it was accompanied by a particular sensation. There is something singularly unique about it which you may not be able to vocalise, but which you instantly recognised when asked to recall being moved by a work of art. You *knew* what you were being asked for, and it is not mundane or ordinary.

We will touch upon many subjects in the course of our journey and deal with them from an intellectual standpoint, but remember that we shall never be far from the realm of your own personal experience. This work was not written purely as an academic exercise; it relates directly to you, and I want you to benefit from it. However remote the concepts appear there is relevance to the individual – a relevance which will become more apparent and more intimate as we progress. We are heading down a path of discovery.

<u>Additional note:</u> if you wish to thoroughly understand this book, you need to understand the words that are used in it. Therefore, if you are unsure of the meanings of any words that you come across, look them up in a dictionary. Obvious, really, yet it is amazing how few people actually do it.

It is advised to follow the book from start to finish, rather than skipping between chapters, as much of the information, particularly in the later stages, builds on what has gone before.

Introduction

There is little doubt that art is a precious commodity and of inestimable value to society. If one were to try and picture a world without art, a bland and dismal vista would no doubt present itself. For some, the negation of art would form a cruel and unusual punishment that would make life unbearable, or at least undesirable. There are no known peoples of Earth who do not engage in artistic pursuit, nor are there any of days gone by, stretching back as far as we have any evidence. The greatest triumphs of man, the glories of past civilisations and the splendour of the natural world, are all to be found embodied, described, engendered, heralded or produced by great works of art. It has played a central role in every major religion. Nothing expresses more about a culture, tradition or civilisation, past or present, than its art.

On an individual level, art touches every person, in one sense or another, and enriches our daily lives. It sees us through the good times and the bad, makes sense of the incomprehensible, provides company when we are inconsolable, characterizes our precious moments, uplifts our spirits and inspires our most profound achievements.

But what is it? What does it do? How does it do it?

If we examine the significance of art down through the ages, we get the impression it was attributed a different role in many societies of the past to that which is recognised today. So before we take a personal look at the relevance of our subject to you in the here and now, let us get a sense of the historical context by taking a whistle-stop tour.

The ancient Chinese civilisation was held together by music, only allowing certain notes to be played at certain times of the day and in certain locations. By their own admission, this stable society only broke down through the infiltration of foreign music into the culture. A similar state of affairs existed with Indian classical music, where a budding musician had to apprentice for twenty years with a master before being allowed to perform in public.

Whether we understand and accept these ideas or not, the ancient Greeks certainly would have, as they attributed a similar status to the arts. In *The Republic*, Plato stated:

> "...any musical innovation is full of danger to the whole State, and ought to be prohibited. When modes of music change, the fundamental laws of the State always change with them."

Aristotle concurred with Plato that there should be laws to govern the nature and character of music, and added:

> "...it is plain that music has the power of producing a certain effect on the moral character of the soul, and if it has the power to do this, it is clear that the young must be directed to music and must be educated in it."

Introduction

Pythagoras defined the fundamental harmonic intervals[1] which have been the basis of the western tonal system used ever since. He went beyond this, however, to draw up a complex map of what he deemed to be the resonant frequencies of the celestial bodies. A whole cult built up around his notion of the "Harmony of the Spheres". Despite the inaccuracies of his calculations, these ideas have reverberated right down the centuries to the present day, where they occasionally resurface in diverse groups, all struggling to compensate for the information that has gone missing or been distorted along the way.

Crossing back over the planet, we discover that the insights of Pythagoras had their roots in far older cultures, as did so much of the knowledge that eventually found its way over to the West. The ancient Sumerian and Babylonian civilisations of the Middle East developed highly sophisticated artistic and musical systems, steeped in symbolism, that were interwoven throughout every aspect of their culture. Examining even a little of these systems leaves the impression that the Pythagoreans were themselves struggling to piece together the scraps of knowledge that had been passed down through the mystery schools of ancient Egypt, and had trickled on into their time.

The Australian Aboriginal people have upheld their deeply embedded tradition through *Songlines*. These Songlines are believed to be the routes taken by their ancient ancestors, criss-crossing the country, when they were creating the land, animals and rule of law for

---

1   Pythagoras noted that two strings of the same length and thickness, when plucked, produce the same note. This is the most basic interval, known as a **unison**. He also noted that a string of exactly half the length produces a note which resonates with the first. This has become known as the interval of an **octave** e.g. if one plays a "C" on a piano, then the next "C" above it, this would be an octave. If a string of 2/3 the length is plucked, another pleasant interval is obtained – the **fifth**, so called because it corresponds to the fifth note of a scale. These ratios can be played going either higher or lower in pitch, and form the Pythagorean Intervals.

human societies. The people of each area are responsible for passing on the sacred creation stories of their respective tracts of land in the form of long song cycles, by which all the history and culture of the region are also passed on. The art works of the Aboriginal people up to the present day are resplendent in visual representations of the Songlines which are so important to them.

Consider the breathtaking feats of architecture of the ancient world, from the Angkor Wat temple in Cambodia to the stepped pyramids of the Maya[2], with their intricate ornamentations, imposing structures and mystifying ingenuity. However they were created, such monumental effort was expended in their production that they must have held a significance well beyond a mere titillation of the senses. The imagery at such locations, often integral to the structures and in plentiful abundance, appears to be encoded with all manner of symbolism, "sacred geometry" embodying fundamental laws of physics and nature, and secret knowledge. Secret, in that we do not know, today, the true meanings and functions that these sites and these works originally held, yet their beauty and power continues to pull millions of visitors to them from all over the globe.

Clearly, much has been lost. This was already being appreciated in the second century AD, when we see the Greek rhetorician Athenaeus regretfully writing:

> *"In olden times the feeling for nobility was always maintained in the art of music, and all its elements skilfully retained the orderly beauty appropriate to them. Today, however, people take up music in a haphazard and irrational manner. The musicians of our day set as the goal of their art success with their audiences."*

---

2 A civilisation which thrived in Mexico and central America, noted for their advanced mathematics, astrology and hieroglyphic script.

Introduction

Those words in the final sentence ring startlingly true today, to the degree that it requires effort to see how matters could once have been any different. We may well ask what goal the people so referred to "in olden times" had of their art? Let us move forward as we attempt to rediscover some answers.

The great cathedrals and churches of Europe abound with aesthetic properties. Built over generations, the person laying the first stone never getting to see its completion, they tell a tale of remarkable dedication. The acoustic properties of some of these buildings are astounding and could not have come about by chance. Visual delights scale from the grand architectural structures and down to the most intricate of decorations. As discussed by James Gleick in his book on Chaos Theory, these design features exhibit a fractal quality in that, however near or far one stands from it, there is sufficient detail to maintain interest. As one approaches, another layer of detail reveals itself at each stage, as in the creations of nature such as trees. This is also true of the interiors, as one approaches the walls, alcoves, ceilings and fixtures. Contemporary buildings seldom have this quality – a square block looks like a square block, no matter the distance from which it is viewed.

It gives one pause to imagine what kind of culture could afford the time and painstaking effort required to accomplish these wonders, let alone envisage their motivation for doing so. Our mechanisation and "advances" should be providing abundance and leisure galore, yet it is in the modern world that buildings are thrown up as quickly and cheaply as possible. Sometimes we hear it suggested that tradesmen were forced to slave away at these constructions by an oppressive Catholic regime, but this does not satisfy as an explanation. People are not suppressed into creating beauty, and these monuments were clearly a labour of love. Exquisite art is not produced by duress, it is produced by passion. The religions and populaces of the day certainly appreciated the power of art.

It was not only the Greek philosophers who studied and commented upon art; it has remained an ever-present subject of debate. If you have had no contact with philosophy, or have the idea that it is a "dead" subject and doesn't mean anything in the "real" world, please think again. The core ideas underlying a culture do more to shape that culture than any other factor. These ideas filter down from the dusty halls of intellectuals, past the rulers and politicians, through the artists, inventors and engineers, reworded by the journalists and town criers, and down into the "common knowledge" and "common values" of the everyday man and woman. You may be surprised to discover the origins of the attitudes which govern every aspect of our daily lives.

The philosopher Immanuel Kant published three critiques in the late seventeen hundreds, in which he sought to separate out reason, right action/moral worth, and art and aesthetics. This splitting of the platonic concepts of truth, beauty and goodness led to the modernity of science and technology, private morals and legal forms, and modern art. J.M. Bernstein traces the effect of this separation, highlighting the significance in that for the first time, art could be viewed as a matter of mere subjective fancy. Lamenting what he describes as "aesthetic alienation", Bernstein issues the warning:

> *"When art loses its critical capacity it ends, will end, for a second time."*

From the same period as Kant, Beethoven, possibly reacting to the Kantian treatment of aesthetics, stated in no less dramatic terms:

> *"I must despise a world which does not know that music is a higher revelation than all wisdom and philosophy"*

To the modern ear these ideas may even appear quaint, but it remains that for the vast majority of man's history, art was granted a much weightier significance. Only in very recent times has the capacity developed to view it frivolously, divorced from truth, and bereft of ethical and cognitive practices.

Today, philosophy is commonly presented as a five-tier hierarchy which places art at the bottom of the pile. In the following order, the hierarchy reads:

1. Metaphysics – the study of existence and the nature of reality
2. Epistemology – the study of knowledge (how do we know about existence and reality?)
3. Ethics – how should we act and what is good?
4. Politics – how should we interact and organise our social affairs?
5. Aesthetics – the nature of beauty and art.

The suggestion is that once one takes a standpoint in one of these categories, it is reflected through the rest. For example, if a person takes the metaphysical standpoint that the whole of reality is simply a figment of their own imagination, they may seek nothing other than their own subjective experience to prove this assertion (epistemology). With this foundation in place, they may adopt a hedonistic lifestyle and take it upon themselves to act however they please (ethics), as the right action is clearly whatever brings them pleasure and, after all, there are no real consequences. Such a mindset would have no qualms about oppressively ruling a nation in a dictatorship and, ultimately, art would simply be a matter of their personal taste.

There is a certain logic to this hierarchical structuring of philosophy, yet it is a logic which only holds once one has already made certain assumptions about the metaphysical and epistemological realms. Without wanting to get too sidetracked at this stage, we shall revisit to these ideas later on once we have accumulated more information to evaluate their validity.

Returning to our historical round-up, and moving into the twentieth century, the year 1917, and the Society of Independent Artists in New York promoted that they would display any work of art in their salon, provided that the artist pay the required fee. Marcel Duchamp, who was a member of that board, submitted an upside-down urinal, entitled *Fountain,* and signed it "R. Mutt, 1917". The society rejected *Fountain,* proclaiming it not to be a true work of art. Duchamp resigned in protest.

This event created a whirlwind of reaction, dividing the world of art in defence or criticism of Duchamp's offering and its subsequent rejection. The confusion that existed on the question of "what is art?" was brought to the fore - a question to which there has been no resolution since, only further confusion. The reverberations continue through to the present day, via a parade of disciples producing similar, or yet more extreme works in Duchampian fashion, in an attempt to test, stretch or obliterate the boundaries.

As we move towards contemporary times, we start to see the effects filter through from the philosophies developed in the wake of Kant. In the intervening years, schools of thought had taken hold which insisted that there is no meaning to anything, or that there is no real way to contact or make sense of reality from our subjective experiences. Now rejecting modernist ideology and adopting the ethos of "anything goes", the world ushered in the postmodern age of general disillusionment with life, and disbelief in existing value systems to effect beneficial change.

Postmodern art movements, which discredited expertise, knowledge and eminence of achievement, fitted hand-in-glove with the instant-fix entertainment culture. They led the drive to embrace the futility and nonsense which surrounds us, accept that both art and life have no meaning, and perhaps we'll enjoy our fifteen minutes of fame.

Is this really the destiny, not only of art, but of the race? Are there no lessons we can learn? Are we to throw up our hands, accept the hopelessness of our fate, and amuse ourselves while we watch the world slide to its inevitable oblivion? Accepting that we can't go back (and shouldn't necessarily wish to), is there a positive way forward?

Bernstein, amongst others, believes that if art can recover some of its rightful status, it can bridge the epistemological chasm that has opened up in our thinking between the subjective and a concept of reality, and thereby restore some sense of value, purpose and worth to people's lives. As he states:

> *"aesthetic discourse contains concepts and terms of analysis, a categorical framework, which, if freed from a confinement in an autonomous aesthetic domain, would open the possibility of encouraging a secular world empowered as a source of meaning beyond the self or subject."*

This is all well and good, but what art are we referring to? Is the art being laudably spoken of above the same art as the glut of over-exposed shallowness being plastered all over every flat or curved surface in our environments? What are we really talking about when we talk of art? If we are to get a sense of its true capabilities, its proper role in society, and the functions that it could and should rightly fulfil, we had better get a grip of what we are going to include under this increasingly catch-all term of "art", lest we attempt to attribute these purposes to everything.

Times have moved on from the days of having to wait for the annual theatre tour to come to the village. With the plethora of multimedia sources on tap for people to browse in their pockets, the majority of which being bland, misleading, trite, degraded or just plain pointless, there is a need for some sorting of the wheat from the chaff. How are people to go about this for themselves, when they may not know where to look, nor indeed what they are looking for?

People instinctively feel the echoes of the past and feel themselves shaken, uplifted and transported by the various art forms they encounter. They sense that art runs deeper than a superfluous piece of amusement; that it has more gravity than airy efforts of attention seeking. It's no wonder they get confused when they see a pile of bricks with a price tag of millions – it serves to alienate them and make them believe they just don't understand the scene. But I would argue that you *can* know all you need to know about the arts, and that, inherently, you probably know more than you realise already.

Having said that, it takes a brave man to attempt a comprehensive definition of art. One of the most influential definitions in modern times comes from George Dickie, (Professor Emeritus of Philosophy at the University of Illinois) as introduced in his *Institutional Theory of Art*. It is quite verbose, but generally boils down to the notion that art is anything which has been conferred the status of art by a member of the "artworld" – that being the art institutions, critics, journalists, historians, philosophers, etc. We thank them for their dedication in this task, but it is doubtful whether we need the "artworld" (if such a body or entity could be clearly defined) to tell us these things. This truth is laid bare by the exercise engaged upon at the beginning of this book – you all *know* what an artistic experience is.

Dickie has appended clarifications to his definition, stating that a work not only has to be credited by the artworld, but that it also has to be an artifact created with the intention of being art. It's difficult to see how much of an improvement this offers. I shan't bother to pick apart this definition as it has more holes than a Swiss cheese, but what is interesting is that it would be accepted at all, not least by scholars. What situation has emerged that would lead educated experts in their field to adopt such an obviously unsatisfactory definition for their most basic term? It is tantamount to an admission of surrender – giving up all hope of delineating it rationally and resorting to: "it is what we say it is".

There are many facets of art, and perhaps many ways to define it. There have been many attempts at definitions and much raging debate has ensued. You may ask, should we be concerned about how we define art? Well, firstly, just from a language point of view, it is important that we use words correctly to communicate what we mean. We could use a generalised term like "creature" to describe a cat. This wouldn't necessarily be wrong, as a cat is a type of creature. But we would likely convey a very ambiguous picture if we were to say "a *creature* was prowling around the house last night".

This is only part of a wider issue of the way in which language affects us and our relationships, as was examined by Alfred Korzybski in his *General Semantics*. The central principal of his work is the idea that "the map is not the territory". When we try to describe something about the world, say, what happened at the breakfast table this morning, we create an abstraction. Our description will be a selective representation of the event, based upon our subjective experience of it. We may say that we had two eggs on toast, a cup of coffee, sat on the far left side of the table, etc., but no matter how detailed we become in our description we will never be able to accurately relate the totality of all that occurred. And someone else who was also present would give a different account from their perspective. When asked about it a week later, we may simply say "I had breakfast" – a further abstraction.

Language itself is such an abstraction. It is a map that we use to describe our territory, a filter through which we view the world, but it will always fall short of conveying pure reality. The word "cup" is a generalised term that will never fully encapsulate that object that you are drinking from and your experience of it. This is not, however, limited to objects and language, but extends to concepts, actions and circumstances, resulting in discrepancies in the understanding of their meaning from one person to another.

The situation becomes more confused when we consider that words carry with them associations and connotations that will vary person to person and circumstance to circumstance. The word "home" will have different significances when spoken to a millionaire, a refugee or a nomad. And if the millionaire becomes bankrupt and ends up on the street it will take on a different significance for him.

When we have words, concepts or topics that over time have accumulated so many associations, thrown at them by so many people that they become culturally ingrained, it is difficult to peer through all these filters to see the reality underneath. Art is one such word and subject.

I believe the scene has become muddied by the inclusion of unnecessary elements into the field of art for which there is no justification. It is my contention that elucidation on the subject of art can be obtained by removing these unwarranted associations, enabling a purer vision of art itself. We need to distinguish what art is *not*, before we can begin to see what it *is*.

How might this be of use? Some examples may help.

When everything pertaining to the spirit, including any cult followings, political movements, etc. are dumped under the banner of "religion", we end up with misleading representations. Cultural, social and racial issues are frequently labelled as religious disputes when they bear little, if any, relation. Throughout history, crusades have slaughtered mercilessly and countless wars have been attributed to the name of religion. Yet I have not read a religious text from any tradition that would condone such actions – quite the opposite in fact. When I have spoken to people from any religion and discussed their faith, killing people has not been a part of it. If one were to enter into a discussion on the topic of religion, and speak only of wars and their consequences, whatever one's beliefs or feelings on the subject, one would be missing the point of religion.

Political systems are an area of massive confusion. There is much debate about what actually constitutes the "right" and "left" in political terms. The Americans trumpet the banner of democracy, yet they are (or are supposed to be) a republic. So many aspects of daily life are coming under the dominion of government, where they have no right to be. Law and order, key economic policy and defence may be legitimate responsibilities of government, however, running television networks, censoring books, internet filtering, and instructing the population on how many fruit and vegetables they should eat each day, stray further into the realm of parenting than politics. Such a motherly handling of a country could benefit on both sides from being stripped down to focus on the essentials. Put another way, we could do with asking what politics *is* and what it *isn't*.

I should add, briefly, that this situation is not just the fault of governments overstepping their mark, or some power-crazed oligarchs seeking to control everyone from shadowy back corridors, but has been occasioned by a general shunning of responsibilities in our daily lives. Although it has been heavily discussed in the halls of philosophy, how many of us have sat down and really thought about what we *do* and what we *don't* want from our governments? Frequent cries of "what are *they* going to do about it?" demand attention from those looking to increase their polling scores, when for the majority of social issues the call should be "what are *we* going to do about it?"

15

Moving on, economics is so riddled with distortions, false concepts, groundless theories and unreliable sources that the basics of the subject have become obfuscated to the point where the majority of people have no clue where money comes from, nor what it is founded upon. This is so much the case that Henry Ford once said:

> *"It is well enough that people of the nation do not understand our banking and monetary system, for if they did, I believe there would be a revolution before tomorrow morning."*

But our subject is art. It will be difficult, if not impossible, to accurately define the essence of art until it has been stripped and laid bare for all to see, and I believe the world will greatly benefit from such a revelation. Art is a distinct entity. It has its own characteristic, its own function, its own purpose, its own role to play in society. It must be divorced from unwarranted alliances and afforded the status and identity it rightly deserves.

We are not here, in this work, going to attempt to define art, and thus fuel the fire and add to the confusion. Another tack shall be taken which aims to clear some of the clouds away to henceforth ensure plain sailing. I don't pretend to have the whole thing sewn up. Naturally, I would not be writing a book such as this if I didn't have some ideas, yet I am neither bold nor stupid enough to announce to the world that I have solved a debate which has troubled the best minds throughout history.

Nor is this work an act of snobbery. I'm not flying the flag for or against any particular genre, tradition or artistic discipline. I am a lover of art, and try to embrace it in as many forms as I am able. And I don't expect you, necessarily, to agree with everything I say. In fact, a degree of argumentation would reassure me that you were engaging with the subject. But I at least hope to provoke some debate on a

Introduction

much-needed topic.

Most of all, I hope that debate takes place with yourself. Whether you be an artist, an art appreciator, or simply someone who is interested or wants to learn, this book can help you to examine what you believe and straighten some things out. Many artists have been misled into focusing on specious goals. With these removed, they are freed up to realign with their objective. Many enthusiasts have been sold down the river by self-serving critics, over-complicating the scene and completely missing the point. Clearing away the false data can serve to dissipate the mystique. Far from taking anything away, such an unveiling should ultimately enable us to love art all the more, whatever our engagement with it.

You may well ask, "how are we to discuss art, if we are to set off at the outset by refusing to define art?" It is a valid question. For the time being, and for the purposes of this work, we shall assume that you, the reader, already have a satisfactorily workable definition of art – that is, workable enough to see us through our current discussion. We are justified in making this assumption as you clearly understood what was being asked of you when the request was made to recall a moment when you were truly touched by a work of art. You *knew* what you were being asked for, didn't you? At the moment, this is all the understanding that is required. As we progress, however, and you give it a little thought, you may find that your understanding blossoms.

And please do not jump (as some unfortunately have) to the retort of "well, if you can't say what art is, then you can't say what it is not either". I shall use the following example to speak for the illogic of this statement. If I were to ask you how many grains of sand there are on Miami beach, you may well answer that you don't know. However, if I were now to assert that the answer is three, you may well protest. Whether or not you have been to Miami beach, you can be quite confident that my answer is an erroneous one. You may not know what

17

the correct answer is, but you know that I'm wrong – it's *not* three.

As a final forewarning, I offer an apology in advance if there be a bias toward music in my writings. I am a lover of many forms of art, so have tried to cover the spectrum evenly. Certainly, any of the points under discussion apply equally to all the arts. Having been a musician all my life, this field provides me with the greatest number of associations and experiences from which to draw, so a tendency to favour this discipline may come through. Hopefully this will not be off-putting for travellers from any field, as you are all most welcome on this journey.

Chapter 1

The First *Not*

Let us begin by considering the following excerpts regarding music, reproduced at length to retain the essence of the picture painted by their authors. The first is taken from the introduction to a small, old book simply entitled "Music" which I discovered years ago in a dusty second-hand book shop:

> "Music, the word we use in our everyday language, is nothing less than the picture of our Beloved. It is because music is the picture of our Beloved that we love music. But the question is, what is our Beloved and where is our Beloved? Our Beloved is that which is our source and our goal; and what we see of our Beloved before our physical eyes is the beauty which is before us; and that part of our Beloved not manifest to our eyes is that inner form of beauty of which our Beloved speaks to us. If only we would listen to the voice of all the beauty that attracts us in any form, we would find that in every aspect it tells us that behind all manifestation is the perfect Spirit, the spirit of wisdom.

...all that we love in colour, line, form or personality belongs to the real beauty, the Beloved of all. And when we trace what attracts us in this beauty which we see in all forms, we shall find that it is the movement of beauty; in other words the music. All forms of nature, for instance the flowers, are perfectly formed and coloured; the planets and stars, the earth, all give the idea of harmony, of music. The whole of nature is breathing; not only the living creatures but all nature; And the sign of life given by this living beauty is music...

...What we call music in our everyday language is only a miniature, which our intelligence has grasped from that music or harmony of the whole universe which is working behind everything, and which is the source and origin of nature. It is because of this that the wise of all ages have considered music to be a sacred art. For in music the seer can see the picture of the whole of the universe; and the wise can interpret the secret and the nature of the working of the whole universe in the realm of music."

(Sufi Inayat Khan, 1914)

The second extract comes from a work of fiction:

"It dawned on Jherek, after a few moments, that this was the most beautiful music he had ever heard. It was profound, stately, and very moving. It hinted at harmonies beyond the harmonies of the physical universe; it spoke of ideals which were magnificent in their sanity, their intensity and their humanity; it took him through despair and he no longer despaired, through pain and he no longer felt pain, through cynicism and he knew exhilaration and hope; it

Chapter 1: The First Not

showed him what was ugly and it was no longer ugly; he was dragged into the deepest chasms of misery only to be lifted higher and higher until his body, mind and feelings were in perfect balance and he knew an immeasurable ecstasy."

(Michael Moorcock,
The Dancers at the End of Time)

Now think of the *Birdie Song, Agadoo, Mr. Blobby, Who Let The Dogs Out?* or *Itsy Bitsy Teenie Weenie Yellow Polka Dot Bikini*. Does something seem amiss? Is there anything that doesn't quite match between these pictures?

No doubt the quoted passages refer to intense artistic experience, perhaps similar to that which you were asked to conjure in the first step. Compare these, if any comparison is possible, to a cartoon in a tabloid newspaper, the latest radio jingle or ditty from the world of "pop music", or an uncouth limerick that would make your Grandmother blush. Notwithstanding that there may be a time and a place for such offerings – you may be a fan of cartoons, pop music and dirty limericks, and that is all well and good – but what is obvious is that we are no longer talking about the same subject. These clearly produce a different class of experience to that of art in its purest sense as depicted above, and it is senseless to even consider them in the same light.

So where can we make the distinction? Is there any way to separate these entities out, or are they, as some schools of thought would have us believe, just different shades of the same gradient scale? There is indeed a division, but one that has become so obscured, the subjects so consistently identified with one another, that it is no longer even noticed or acknowledged. Yet once the spotlight is turned upon it, the confusions start to melt away with dazzling clarity, as we consider our first *not:*

Art is *not* entertainment.

There is no assertion being made here that a work of art cannot be entertaining, or that a piece of entertainment cannot have an artistic value, but that they are individual concepts with their own ends. That they may bleed into one another is, from one perspective, unfortunate, and that they have become all but synonymous in our modern culture is disastrous. Any form of entertainment is deemed to be art, which, as will soon be shown, it is clearly not. The merit of any work of art is judged on the degree to which it entertains, which is not only an unfair index of the work, but tends to drive away any genuine artistic content in the attempt to satisfy the condition.

Entertainment fulfils a wonderful role in providing us with joy, amusement, and often much-needed distraction from the daily toils of life. He who can captivate an audience, make us laugh, help to wile away an otherwise dreary winter's evening, is a valued individual who should be well rewarded. But the function that he fulfils is different to that of an artist. They have different purposes and different ends.

How does one distinguish these ends? Upon what basis am I asserting this schism? How do I know that one even exists? I refer you to your own Prime Experience, and that of an event that you would consider wholly entertainment. Are they the same? Do they hold the same significance for you? Could you even categorise them as the same subject?

By this reasoning, it may be asked, is there then music, painting, poetry and theatre which is not art? We would have to conclude that there is. Let it be understood, this does not infer that such works are of no value. Indeed, it is not even derogatory. All that is asked for is that we consider a work in a context that is appropriate, with the right frame of reference.

If we are to consider all painting as art, including painting a wall or respraying a car, then your local decorator ought to put his prices up. Music is an art form, but is all music art? Radio jingles? Whistling in the bathtub? Ice cream van tunes? Karaoke? When I am engaged as a musician, it is sometimes as an entertainer, and others as an artist. Sure, I am going through the motions of performing with a group of musicians on both occasions, but the roles are different. There may be some crossover, but if you have any experience of this, or any artistic field, it is an interesting exercise to go through one's list of jobs and see if they fall more heavily into one category or another. It is usually quite clear.

The glitz and the glamour and the "smile for the camera" are the domain of Show Business. Artists are notoriously poor at the "business side" of art: the marketing, promotion, finance, distribution, sales, reviews, product placement, market research, etc. But this is an illusion. There is no "business side" to art. That is just business. That is the entertainments industry at work.

A most unsavoury element has come about through this industry which may serve as an example. After paying through the nose from an online exchange you finally managed to get tickets for the sold-out concert that you've been looking forward to for weeks. This is going to be the event of the year. It dominates your social conversations and increasingly your thoughts as the big day arrives. One of your favourite groups of all time are coming to your home country at last. You immediately book the train rides to the city and a hotel for the weekend – just as well you've done all that overtime recently to cover the costs.

You've got yourself dressed up, queued for hours, finally shuffled into the arena and fought for a place that affords you a view of the stage. Then, the blazing lights go on, the crowd cheers, the massive sound system cranks up, and you hear...   ...the recording coming from the mixing desk.

The posters were accurate, albeit carefully worded. They all enticed you to "Come and see (_____) perform live!" They didn't say that you were going to *hear* (_____) perform live. What you actually watched was a bunch of entertainers miming to a tape.

If you think this kind of thing is rare, then I'm afraid you are sorely mistaken. It has been standard practice for TV performances for some time, and for the majority of larger scale concerts most, if not all, of what you hear coming from the speakers will be a recording. This practice is also filtering down to some smaller gigs, especially where there is commercial interest or some concern over image. The record companies don't want anything other than a perfect reproduction to be put out, as this would be bad PR and might affect record sales.

Another factor is also being concealed. I know of a lady, we'll call her Julie, who was a dancer. She was approached by some people at a performance who said they liked the look of her, and wondered if she wanted to be a pop star. Julie said she had never done any singing, and never had any intention of being a singer. That, it was replied, didn't matter – was she interested? Julie decided to go along with it and see what happened, so after exchanging contact details she went for an interview later that week.

To briefly summarise what happened from there, she signed a contract with a record company. The songwriters employed by the company provided some songs, music was recorded by session musicians, collecting their one-off studio fee, and the vocals were similarly recorded by a girl who does a lot of recording in studios – not by Julie. Apparently the studio vocalist didn't share the dancer's physique, and didn't have a face that fit the camera. The camera, that is, which Julie was now performing in front of to film the music videos, and subsequently the TV appearances and magazine features to promote the new releases.

Without knowing what had hit her and before she managed to stop and catch a breath, Julie found herself all over the radio and in the charts. She needed to do some "live" concerts, so received coaching in order to do a convincing job of miming along to the records. Already being a star, she bypassed the smaller venues and launched straight onto stages at major concert halls and arenas. After several years of touring around Europe and America on this circuit, with a couple of albums and a number of hit singles to her name, Julie was phased out of the scene to make way for the next bright and shiny star on the conveyor belt, and she retired from the pop world without ever singing a note.

Back in the 80's, a big media storm was generated over the pop group *Milli Vanilli* who, after having several hit records with accompanying music videos, were unmasked as imposters. They weren't the singers of their chart-topping songs. They had posed for the photo shoots, acted in the videos and mimed through the "live" performances, but the vocals were all recorded by completely different people. A couple of other high profile examples were brought to light in that era, although we seldom hear of this practice nowadays, giving the impression that these were freak and shameful isolated occurrences. If only it were true. Julie is not the only example that I personally know of, and I am no insider in the business. I have spoken to some who are, however, and they assured me that the practice is widespread – now more so than ever.

After talking to people, observing them, and seeing their reactions, I have had to re-evaluate my thinking on this subject. I used to be outraged at how scandalous it all was, distraught at the degradation of art, and longed for a way to enlighten the masses to the injustice and the sham, and to overthrow the whole confounded show. Reflecting on it now, this attitude may be idealistic, but it is also rather unbalanced.

What became apparent to me (shockingly, at first) was that for many concert goes, or folk who would watch such performances on TV, share video clips on social media, etc., it didn't even bother them when they were told the truth. Many were quite accepting of the fact and some already had the idea that this sort of thing was the norm anyway.

My initial appraisal of such reactions was that they have become so numbed to the world of canned entertainment, so conditioned to the fakery and shallowness pumped at them from every angle, that they just accepted that is the way things are and there is nothing to be done about it. But even this appraisal is unreasonable. If someone wants to go to one of these concerts, and they can still enjoy it under those circumstances, and come away talking about how wonderful it all was, then who am I to say there is anything wrong with that? After all, some of these shows can be a real spectacle, with all the laser lights and fireworks, so we can't necessarily even claim that they are not offering good value for money.

Yet this conclusion still didn't sit too well with me, so upon further reflection, I weeded out the two elements that made it unacceptable, and which if handled appropriately would make the whole situation perfectly justifiable. Firstly, what disturbs me is the deceit. The truth about what is being performed, what is not being performed, by whom, and when, should be made public. If it were all out in the open and someone decided they wanted to go to the concert, knowing what they were getting, and were prepared to pay the required fee, then so be it. Let them go and enjoy themselves.

The other issue is that we need to have an understanding of what this kind of activity is. The performers on that stage could be described as entertainers, and they may be very great entertainers, but they cannot be described as artists. The performance as a whole may be great entertainment, thoroughly satisfying the entire audience, but it is not art. Anyone who believes themselves to be producing art while they are faking must have become so far removed from what they are doing as to be wholly disassociated from the subject. They could benefit from taking a step back, examining their motives and aligning themselves with some basics.

"Ghost writers", from what I understand, sometimes fall into the same category. An interview with an international cricketer comes to mind, in which he was asked to comment on his newly-released autobiography. He replied "I haven't read it yet, but I'm looking forward to doing so".

We might also include printed copies of paintings, but these, at least, do not usually pretend to be the genuine article. Forgeries, plagiarisers and possibly even body doubles would come under a different bracket again. Exact parallels to the fabrication phenomenon may not be so obvious in the other arts, but in all are to be found the separate aspects of art and entertainment which perform separate functions.

In the field of entertainment, we have the parade of circus acts: the daring lion tamer, the clown with all his antics, the herculean strong man. An acrobat is going through an extremely skilful, yet mechanical routine, and is largely an entertainer. Same goes for the Limbo dancer and the juggling act. We could include feats of mental agility, like the memory man who can recite a phone book or calculate lightening speed arithmetic. These performances are delivered in a traditional spirit of showmanship. The familiar atmosphere they arouse has widespread appeal, and also unites them in a common orientation. Take a minute to see if you can think of some examples of painting, theatre, music, sculpture, literature or poetry which produce the same kind of atmosphere, or that share a resemblance to this kind of activity. See if there are any that grab your attention in a similar way, or give you the same kind of feeling. If you are stuck, you might begin by considering imagery or sounds that might accompany such acts.

If you read a lot of literature, there are probably many books which have provided you with enjoyment, and which you may be happy to read again if you had spare time to kill. But your favourite books are likely to have given you more than that. They hold a place for you which couldn't be described as merely whiling away the hours. You were engaged in something important in its own right, when you read that book, and it remains important to you now.

A similar appraisal could be made for film. Sure, it may be a favourite movie to put on when your friends come round for a fun evening. You stack up all the drinks and snacks, and laugh harder at it now, on it's fourteenth replay, than you did when you first watched it. But it is unlikely to be the one you were thinking about for your Prime Experience.

This is a little difficult to judge, however, as media with the duration of a film, meandering through various plots and backdrops, may ebb and flow between passages that hold different functions. They tend to eddy and swell around one pool or the other in the majority, but there may be one truly artistic moment in an otherwise exclusively entertaining production.

Video games are a curious one. On the surface of it, and certainly for the majority of their history, one would consider them pure entertainment. However, whether you are interested in playing such games or not, the immersive, aesthetic virtual worlds that some of these all-embracive creations now portray would certainly be capable of producing *bona fide* artistic experiences. A serious amount of work goes into their thoughtfully composed sound tracks, captivating storylines and breathtaking visual scenery and effects.

Conversely, there is no need to expound on the formulaic poems found in greetings cards. They could hardly be said to rival Keats or Tennyson.

OK, you may not be convinced without a little more explanation. I shall attempt to provide some. We may have difficulty in encapsulating a definition for art, but it is a bit easier to locate one for entertainment. Here is the Oxford English Dictionary:

> *"the action of providing or being provided with amusement or enjoyment"*

This would fit our daily soaps and sitcoms, the cartoons on the back of the newspaper, magazine articles, those funny little clips popping up on "social media", party songs and karaoke. But what about your Prime Experience? I would hazard a guess that "provided with amusement or enjoyment" doesn't cut it. I'll bet you got something else out of it.

Just to see how these two terms have become confused, take a look at this definition of "art" from the Cambridge Dictionary:

> *"the making or doing of something whose purpose is to bring pleasure to people through their enjoyment of what is beautiful and interesting"*

Not a great deal of difference there. But again, I'm sure there's a gulf between that and describing your Prime Experience. So we're clear there is a distinction. We may only be examining extremes thus far, but we can try and close in on a demarcation point, and we may start to see that there is more daylight between these two than we originally thought. Let's try another couple of definitions for entertainment, firstly from the omniscient Wikipedia:

> *"a form of activity that holds the attention and interest of an audience, or gives pleasure and delight"*

Recall the quote from Athenaeus in the introduction, lamenting the "success with their audiences" that was orienting the misguided musicians of the day, and compare this with the "holding the attention and interest of an audience" above. It seems clear that Athenaeus feared they had become entertainers rather than artists. But make no mistake, if you are being paid as an entertainer, then you had better have success with your audiences, or you are not doing your job.

The second definition comes from dictionary.com:

> *"Agreeable occupation for the mind; diversion"*

"Occupation for the mind" is probably quite accurate for entertainment. But what of *stimulation* for the mind? There we enter a different category. We may seek a diversion to help us forget a stressful day. If you want something to amuse you for a couple of hours, to escape from the hustle and bustle or to fill up the odd bit of spare time, entertainment is probably the answer. A distraction is a motion away from something. Although, real elucidation and edification is more likely to come from an enticement – a motion towards. It might show you a journey, but does it take you on one?

We may need to shed a few more *nots* before getting to the heart of this matter, but for now, a potential basis upon which to explain the directional difference between art and entertainment shall be suggested. This is offered for consideration, rather than asserted as immutable law, as there may be more than one paradigm to explain the relationship. For excursions such as these, we will be discussing some characteristics of art rather than attempting to define exactly what it is.

A topic, similar in some respects to art, upon which there is no consensus of opinion, is that of *life* – what is *life*? This is another age-old debate that we are not likely to resolve here, but again, for our purposes, we don't have to. What we do need to acknowledge is that it exists. The level of understanding we require is to observe a new born baby and a corpse, and to be able to recognise that there is a difference. There is some intrinsic quality possessed by that baby that the corpse doesn't have. Science, not through want of trying, has not been able to come up with an explanation for what that is, and the topic has divided philosophers for centuries.

Whatever the ultimate truth of it may be, we are going to go with a general understanding for our discussion. There is something that makes alive things alive, and we can observe that there are other things which don't have it which are apparently dead – or, more accurately, simply *not* alive. So we have a rough dividing line between the purely physical elements in the world around us and this other quality which appears to, amongst other possible activities, animate some of the physical things around us. This has been called different things in the past, the *elan vital,* consciousness, the spiritual realm, Chi/Tao, The Force of the Jedi, the universal mind, the hand of God and the Holy Ghost, although we must be wary that this container doesn't end up as a dumping ground for every ounce of enlightenment in an incense stick or Valium-induced apparition of Auntie Mabel in the sky. Many labels could be attributed to these two categories, but we are just going to call them the *physical universe* and *life*.

And that is as far as we are going to go with descriptions. All that is left now is to point out that entertainment, along with other activities, directs a person to the physical universe. Art aligns a person with life. Entertainment may serve as a distraction from a part of the physical universe, the escape from the dreary boredom of the factory floor, but it does so by orienting one to another part of the physical universe and fixing their attention there. Art has other cards up its sleeve. What they are and how it deals its hand is something we shall speculate on in due course. Henry Moore offered these words:

> *"If an artist tries consciously to do something to others, it is to stretch their eyes, their thoughts, to something they would not see or feel if the artist had not done it. To do this, he has to stretch his own first."*

Real art ascends one to another plane; entertainment motions away from the spirit and allies one to the physical universe. One transcends the physical universe, the other pushes you further into it. Art gives one a sense of something beyond – it really is not of this world. It is like an image of a reality long-since forgotten; a passage to a far away land; a portal to a higher existence. It's a glimmer of what *could* be.

True art derives its power from the dance it performs along the line between imagination and understanding. It is not reducible simply to knowledge, as it is beyond knowledge – it deals with the cutting edge out in front of which the knowledge of tomorrow is derived. It is this area that it stimulates and this interplay between imagination and understanding which it directs someone towards.

That which exists purely in the realm of knowledge is therefore not art. If it succeeds in absorbing attention it could best be described as entertainment. If it seeks to pretty up the physical universe a little, like the picture hung on the wall just to make the room look a bit nicer, it is not fulfilling an artistic role.

We will return to these ideas later and hopefully shed a little more light, but for now it would be a worthwhile exercise to start taking stock of what you are viewing, by whatever medium, and seeing if it leans more towards one category or another – art or entertainment. If you need some help, make a comparison with your Prime Experience. What did it give you? And does this offering before you provide the same?

You may believe that to be an unfair or inappropriate comparison, as an artistic experience can take different forms, and not all may be as powerful as the one you brought to mind. If this is an issue, perhaps recall two or three other occasions when a work of art rocked your world – real good ones. Is there any kind of common thread running between them? Some particular feeling or quality accompanying those moments? This may not be an exact science, so don't go banging your head against it for too long if it starts to get tough. But you might have some interesting realisations along the way.

Eleven Things That Art is Not

Chapter 2

The Second *Not*

How often have you entered into a discussion like the following: who is the best painter? Is Beethoven better than Mozart? What's the greatest play ever written? Such conversations seldom go anywhere intelligent or end up in any purposeful conclusion. This is because they are essentially flawed as topics for argument, and their flaw is a symptom of a disease with which the world of art is sorely afflicted. So pervasive is this affliction, so deeply ingrained, so commonplace, that it is now scarcely even noticed.

Art is *not* a competition.

It simply cannot be referred to on those terms, and any attempts to turn it into one are a detraction from art itself. This has not stopped an endless parade of people from trying, but with each attempt all they produce is yet more befuddlement. It is not a trifling matter which can be passed off as "just a bit of fun". I call it a disease as a disease it is, with definite, damaging consequences.

There is nothing wrong with competition. Indeed, it is often healthy and can provide amusement. But if you want competition, then play a sport – that's what it is for. Or play chess, pub quizzes, video games, tiddly-winks, etc. There are no shortage of opportunities to test your skills against those of your fellow man. But do not try to make a competition of art. It is not its function, not its purpose.

And there are many ways in which sides are drawn up and pitted against each other in the arts: which is the best work of art, who is the best artist, which is the best style, genre or period, which is the greatest form of art. Let's examine each in turn to see if there is any merit in them.

Art work versus art work

In the world of sports a race can be timed, a jump measured, and a points total tallied. The rules of the game are known at the outset. One knows what one is striving for and the exact criteria upon which they will be judged. The same cannot be said for a work of art. And if one does head into the production of a piece with the intention of fulfilling certain criteria, the result is usually unsatisfactory. The boxes might all be ticked, but is there a spark of magic? The essential nature of art does not surrender to judgement.

What criteria should one use to judge works of art? For any entity to be categorically stated as "better" than any other entity requires statistical analysis. Which statistic are we to analyse? Any that are proposed either fail to capture the essence of the artistic experience, or miss the point entirely. We can therefore break down this section further into a summary of the usual offerings and potential candidates, along with their respective shortcomings. Dealing with these now paves the way for our future explorations and hopefully puts them to bed once and for all.

– *The physical properties*

This should prove a simple one to dispense with for starters. Can we say that one play is better than another play if it is longer? No. If one sculpture is bigger than another, does this assure its superiority? Hardly. How about if a book is leather-bound and embossed in gold leaf as opposed to a shabby paperback?

A comment often heard from people seeing the Mona Lisa for the first time is: "it isn't as big as I thought it was going to be". One of the most famous paintings of all time, and it's relatively small.

It doesn't require much mental ingenuity to fathom that the size of the stage doesn't bestow a higher status upon a play. When we are dealing with art, we are dealing with a quality outside of physical proportions.

– *Technical complexity*

Poets using the longest possible words don't always make for pleasant reading. Intensely intricate choreography may provide a challenge for the dancers and a spectacle for the audience, but gives no guarantee of artistic merit. The impression may be closer to organised chaos than beauty.

Great works are simply not produced by prescriptions from a text book. Any works that are founded on this basis end up appearing as contrived as they actually are. A million notes does not guarantee a masterpiece. In any art form, the simplest things are often the most effective.

Although, there is still something to be said for technical form, and an intricately woven composition can be both stimulating and provoking. So to provide a balance, let us deal with the trite expression so commonly misused around all the arts: less is more.

The statement itself is an oversimplification. True, it is what you leave out that is often more important than what you put in, but the reductio ad absurdum of "less is more" in art would be to produce nothing. This may have some ultimate truth in a paradoxical universe of opposite extremes meeting in some spiralistic fusion point, and tolerance of nothingness may be an absolute virtue, but it is not very helpful to us in our attempts to produce works of art. It indicates that we have a piece missing from this puzzle. Besides, I would be sceptical of anyone purporting to have produced a pure nothingness.

What confounds us about beautifully simplistic creations is how they can say so much without explicitly describing it all. It is the quality of economy. That which is provided has to be suggestive; it has to lead one on a trail of completing that which has been omitted. You have to entice participation.

Less isn't more. Less is just less. To *imply* more though providing less, is more.

Overall, technique furnishes tools with which to make works of art, but it is neither the art itself, nor can it tell us a great deal about it.

– *Originality*

So you have two original architectural designs in front of you. But is one more original than the other? And if so, how much more original? Could we put a percentage on it? "Well, I've not seen that type of guttering before, but those balconies look fairly standard, and windows are just *so* last millennium".

To say something is original implies that it is novel, unusual, fresh, or basically distinct from what has gone before. In order to distinguish this, it follows that one must have a familiarity with what has gone before. Yet this is a relative commodity. "Unfamiliar to whom?", we might ask. An exact replica of a well-known item is not likely to derive much interest. However we must not be too quick to assume that total originality is desirable, even if it were attainable. There has to be some kind of agreement involved for the recipient to make a connection with the offering. Anything too far out of the box is not going to meet with any recognition, and therefore will also derive no interest. It will be seen as purely alien or chaotic or not even be acknowledged. Part of the great skill of the creator is to take what is known and show it in a new light, not to try and deal in only what is unknown.

Sometimes, new ideas, movements and trends take a while to gain acceptance, in any field of endeavour. Painters are notorious for becoming famous after their death, as many scientists are later hailed as geniuses who were ridiculed in their day. It would be harsh to condemn a radically unconventional artwork that may simply be well ahead of its time.

Sticking to the present, for now, a scale is suggested, which, at either end of total unfamiliarity or complete familiarity, yields no positive result. We could plot interest against familiarity to imagine a graph of "desirable originality" (see fig.1). Perhaps we would get a bell-shaped curve, yet we could not assign any quantitative values to accurately describe this relationship. One could argue that the target of the criteria of originality should reflect the "Proximity to the Point of Optimum Originality". But we would still be at a loss as to a unit of measurement. Even if this could be tied down, the goalposts would shift for each individual exposed to the work, as what is familiar to one may not be familiar to another. So for each judge making an assessment of the piece we would have a new graph and therefore a new "optimum point" at which to aim.

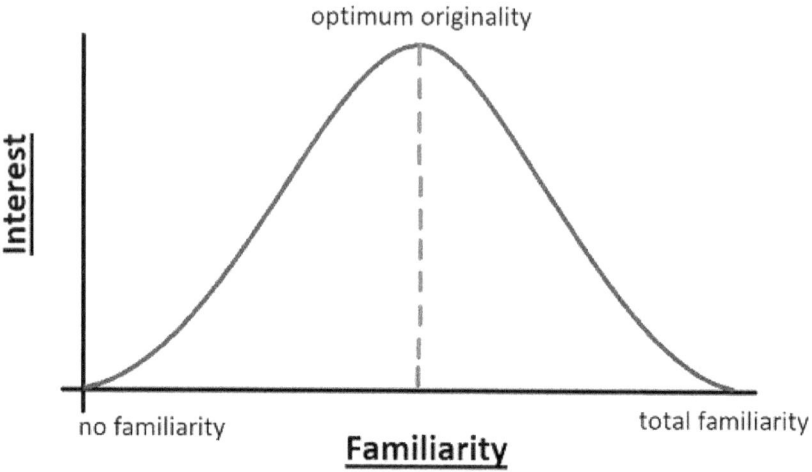

Fig.1 Graph showing imagined level of "desirable originality".

We also have to ask, is an artist expected to have encountered and know of everything, past or current, anywhere in the world, in their chosen field? This seems unreasonable. Are we really to expect an artist to set to work by listing out all the different extant works of art, then determine to do nothing like any of them? What an imposition! *That* is a barrier to creativity if ever there were one. Great works of art are not produced in this fashion. This is also the danger facing art and artists from the ever-growing global behemoth of Copyright law.

The underlying principal of assessing by originality contains an unjustified presupposition that it is a worthy factor in attributing value. Certainly, we like to see new ideas come to the fore, but this is something that occurs as a natural progression of the art form as a whole. As in the sciences, where new advances are built upon the discoveries of yesteryear, an art form evolves, its exponents adding to, modifying, countering, reflecting on, combining and expanding that which has gone before. Themes, concepts and ideas are bound to be borrowed and reused. It is only in the modern age of overly-inflated copyright laws, seeking to protect corporate interests, that words or notes can be "stolen". Bach or Mozart wouldn't have understood such an attitude.

We also must consider the documented phenomenon of inventions and discoveries appearing simultaneously in different parts of the world, and its parallel in the arts. Some put this down to the conditions being "ripe" for the discovery, others attribute a "collective consciousness" of which we are all interlinked, but whatever we deem to be the cause, the data collected suggests that this situation is the norm rather than the odd freak coincidence. Ogburn and Thomas published 150 examples of simultaneously-produced inventions in 1922, and Merton reveals how 32 of Lord Kelvin's discoveries were independently made by others, concluding that it is the dominant pattern rather than a subsidiary one. Yet this does not diminish the brilliance of those inventors, scientists and artists, nor the products of their efforts. The times may have been ready for a breakthrough, but someone still had to make that breakthrough. It just means we have no reliable basis for comparison.

Copyright law was founded several centuries ago with the intention of encouraging the individual artist to produce new works. It no longer performs this function and exists almost entirely to support major conglomerate businesses, and in effect does more to stifle new creative endeavours than empower them. Not wishing to get sidetracked with this issue, however, let's move onto another.

Crowds still flock to see exhibitions of Rembrandt and Michaelangelo. They pack theatres to watch performances of Shakespeare. Concert halls sell out for programmes of Vivaldi and Beethoven. There is nothing new in these works. The audiences know what they are going to get and may have been to see them many times. A work that is centuries old can still appear fresh and new. Tracing back further, how many visitors are received in Greece and Rome each year, hoping to catch sight of the remaining jewels of those long-gone civilisations? And what of the ancient monuments mentioned in the introduction?

One may argue that such works were original in their time. This may, or may not be true, depending on the subject in hand and which perspective we are viewing it from. The point is, they are not original now, and the years have only added to them an extra mystique, like the ageing of a fine vintage, and done nothing to reduce their majesty and appeal. Why do we always have to have something new? A watercolour landscape is not a new idea, but it can still be breathtaking.

There is the case of a direct copying or plagiarising of a work to consider. We could simply argue that they haven't created it, so cannot claim it as theirs. It's fifty percent mental, at least, and they haven't done the mental part if it is merely copied. But if they came up with the idea themselves, then what could we say is wrong with it? This point would be impossible to monitor, but then again, that *is* the point under consideration!

Thus we can see that originality, whether deemed essential or desirable or not, is not something that can be measured.

– *Composition/design*

We can analyse a piece of music and say which harmonic

structure is employed in it, or show the adherence to the Golden Mean and colour wheel in a painting. But these are all analytical tools that are imposed upon the piece after the event.

The same mistake is made in the sciences, where we speak of universal laws and talk of the elements of nature "obeying" these laws. They do no such thing. When we adopt a philosophy, we choose to view the world through that framework. If it be a scientific one, we have selected out certain facts with which we align our view of reality. We have constructed a way of thinking about physical phenomena that enable us to make use of them and predict certain other phenomena. But there are a multitude of viewpoints with which to view the physical universe, and an inestimable number of facts that could be selected out for our mental construct. To say that the universe is now following *our* idea of what it is doing, is not only inaccurate but extremely conceited. The universe is just doing what it is doing. It is *us* who are struggling to find a way to comprehend it.

Similarly, an artist doesn't follow any laws. They simply create what they create because that is what seems right to them. They may well "break with tradition" and do something unconventional, but this would again be a reverse view of the situation. As Debussy put it: "Works of art make rules, rules do not make works of art". The conventions are the tools of the analyst, struggling to understand how such a great effect is produced by the segment that strays across the bounds of conventional wisdom. For this reason, a composition or design cannot be "wrong", and if it cannot be said to be right or wrong, it cannot be said to be any better or worse.

– *Aesthetic quality*

OK, I throw my hands up at this one. You will find this category listed under the judging criteria for many literature, painting, poetry and musical competitions, but I am at a total loss to know how anyone could attribute a numerical value to such a concept. If any of you out there could furnish me with a plausible answer I would love to hear from you.

– *Longevity*

Some pieces are said to have "stood the test of time". It's something that we feel to be true, but it's not exactly clear what is meant by this. Some medieval chants have survived and continue to be performed and recorded. In the modern era, particularly since the digital revolution, nearly all works are recorded in one form or another. If we can tick the longevity box by having a reproduction of it existing in some format somewhere, then we shall have more ticks than all the clocks in Switzerland.

Imagine that an archaeological dig on the outskirts of the Giza Plateau[3] unearths a sculpted stone head, which is cleaned up and unquestionably dispatched for display in a museum. We could say that it has "stood the test of time" - thousands of years of it. But what test is it supposed to have passed – whether it is old? For all we know it could have been used by the Pharaohs of Egypt as a door stop. Now it is elevated to the status of a jewel of antiquity.

It is not enough for it merely to have survived. It wouldn't help to add that a work should still have some significance, as this is just introducing another nebulous term. Perhaps we could say it still needs to be appreciated, although, it is more often than not the case that if you once liked a piece of art, music, etc., that you will always have some level of affinity for it. You may have moved on from there and involve yourself in a completely different scene nowadays, but there is

---

3 The Giza Plateau is an area of desert on the outskirts of Cairo, Egypt, upon which the three Great Pyramids and the Great Sphinx are situated.

not much that you would whole-heartedly turn your back on once you have developed a bond with it.

There obviously also remains the question of how to judge a new creation that hasn't had any time to test it. The criteria simply doesn't apply.

It is a truism that "a great work of art is always a great work of art". Some styles, however, through no fault of their own, may now appear to us as dated, and lack the appeal that they once had. This does not belittle the fact that they were once great.

We therefore have no test upon which we can rely. Can old father time sit us on his knee and explain to us why a droll, inconsequential drizzle of mundanity, that has bored its way through generations, is better than a bolt which shook the world in a short and finite period of time?

– *Influence*

Some works of art are cited as having spawned whole movements or genres. On closer inspection, however, this is seldom the case. Many factors contribute towards a culture, and the factors which lead to the production of the said work also contributed to what followed in its wake.

In using this yardstick we also suffer from clarity. Something could be influential in many ways – culturally, politically, philosophically, etc. It could also have a positive or a detrimental influence, and it is not always easy to determine which. It would be difficult to make a case for the greatness of a work of art based on influence, if its overall contribution were a destructive one.

– *Monetary value/commercial potential*

There are numerous factors influencing the revenue derived from a work of art, the vast majority of which having nothing whatsoever to do with the artwork itself, meaning that any conclusion thus drawn is dubious. We shall only touch lightly on a couple of these as the reader will no doubt perceive the pointlessness of the task.

Paintings are bought and sold as investments and are thus subject to the usual market forces of any valuable commodity. The governance of supply and demand is germane to economics and tells us little about the item in question. Antiques and sculptures go in and out of fashion and their prices fluctuate accordingly. To take a snapshot of the current state of the market at any given point in time, and subsequently assign that value to the pieces under consideration, is an exercise in randomness.

The quoted figures that are grossed at the box office escalate with each new blockbuster release. Even if these figures were reliable, what would they really tell us? They tell us how many people were convinced to go to the cinema to see the film. If anything, this would be an indication of the success of the marketing campaign. And this is the crux of any issue we bring up under the heading of money: when we talk of money, we talk of business, and not art.

– *Popularity*

Another common method is to ascribe value by popular vote. It's an attractive concept, but sadly doesn't work in practice. When the general public are asked to judge an art competition, the winning picture is invariably a kitten playing with a ball of wool. What are they judging it on? The painting, or the fact that they like cute cats? What criteria do *they* use to assign worth, and why would they be any more valid than the ones we are going over here?

The popular vote always tends toward the lowest common denominator. The main problem with this is that emerging art forms, genres and styles may take some time to gain acceptance. They will, if there is any genuine originality in them, be to a degree out of reality with the average. Too much of a degree and they are not likely to gain attention at all. But some forms of art take some conditioning; they take some getting used to before one might start to appreciate them. The popular vote doesn't allow for this. It is a vote on what is already familiar and grooved in with the masses.

> *"You can only make art that talks to the masses when you have nothing to say to them."*
>
> *(Andre Malraux)*

Also, we here run into an overwhelmingly influential factor which makes "popularity" a meaningless index. That is the factor of exposure. Sure, plenty of people gave it the vote for best animation after it was played on prime-time TV and appeared on mugs, fluffy toys, boxer shorts and all the other merchandise. But what about all the fantastic pieces of animation that nobody ever gets to see?

The influence of mass marketing and dominance of media coverage are plain to anyone who takes an honest look at it. We cannot rely on the products of this machine as being a worthy representation of the cream of the creative wealth of our nations. The organisations involved foster the primary motive of making money, not of producing great works of art. And they have proven time and time again that, with enough money behind them, you can make *anyone* famous, and *for anything.*

Fortunately, modern developments, particularly with the rise of the internet, are changing the state of play in this regard. Certainly there are positives and negatives to the digital revolution, but one thing it has given us is the awareness of the myriad diversities and staggering strength in depth of creative genius that the world possesses. No more can we be convinced, if we are prepared to do even a trifling amount of research, that there be only a handful at the top of their profession.

By the way, the term "pop music" and the phrase "it's called pop music because it's popular" were invented and deliberately spread through the society by the Psychiatrists at the Tavistock Institute for Human Relations as part of a social experiment. If you have ever used this phrase then you certainly fell for it.

Getting back to the point in hand, popularity doesn't advance us in the cause of tying down art to the click of a stopwatch. Let us consider a scenario:

Sculptor A lives in the city. He produces Sculpture A which is launched, to the clink of champagne glasses and the nibbling of canapés, as part of an exhibition in a fashionable down-town gallery. Local business folk and wannabe celebs mingle in superficial sincerity as they carefully contrive carefree conversations within range of the media crocodiles, who are busily snapping away to capture the centre page spreads. The party is hailed as a great success. Attendees proclaim it to have been "stimulating", "profound", "exciting", and some of them had even gotten around to looking at the sculptures, which they found "nice".

Sculptor B lives at the foot of a mountain. She lives a solitary life; some might even say recluse. Yet not that she would consider it so, having the company of the birds, the trees, the misty first rays of sunshine tentatively reaching over the mountain, and the hammer and chisel with which she thoughtfully fashions Sculpture B out of the rescued remains of the thunderstruck oak from the lakeside.

A weary traveller, on his final wandering search for meaning in his tear-drenched existence, happens upon the newly erected Sculpture B at the entrance to the wood, and, gazing in glass-eyed wonderment, is so moved by its beauty that he is wrenched from the depths of depression, awakened to the shimmering transparency of his ghostly hauntings, and transported from his nightmare into a dream. After the fleet-footed hours have flown down the road of reverie, the traveller bids farewell to the wood-side sanctuary and sets off down the road of regeneration, with an internal spark which from that moment on would grow into the blaze of purposeful desire to go on living.

So which takes the prize? Sculpture A or Sculpture B? The popular vote registers no contest – it's Sculpture A every time. If we are to measure by this yardstick then it is of no consideration that thousands were exposed to Sculpture A, of which a few hundred said they liked it and with which perhaps a dozen had any genuine connection. It's possible that the lonely traveller be the only person (other than its creator) to ever set eyes on Sculpture B, but the ballots have been tallied: it's several hundred to one. And that's not including the legion of bandwaggoners professing to be a follower of Sculptor A's work without ever actually seeing any of it.

And who knows – they may be right! Perhaps some adherents of Sculpture A had earth-shattering experiences, and other visitors to the wood were disgusted by the ugly pile of logs rotting in the muddy clearing, gathering toadstools. The point is, this index doesn't tell us anything.

So how about measuring the percentage of people who liked the work, after having been exposed to it? Heavy laurels (accompanied by suspicious disbelief) to anyone who would propose a watertight method for monitoring that statistic. And any such attempt would be plagued by similar difficulties in breaking it down. To illustrate:

Bill: *"Fred? Have you finished the latest survey yet?*

Fred: *"Yes Bill. Ran something like this:*

- *2% were consumed in ecstatic rapture,*
- *16% loved some of it, liked bits of it, and hated the rest,*
- *23% liked it, but said that the artist could do better,*
- *34% didn't like it and said that they could do better,*
- *15% would only bring it out to keep the mother-in-law quiet when she comes round to visit, and...*
- *6% choked on their criticisms and ended up in intensive care at the local hospital."*

Bill: *"I'm no mathematician, but I believe that totals to 96%."*

Fred: *"Yes Bill. The other 4% are made up of those who couldn't be reached, had been advised by their lawyers not to comment, weren't credible as they had only seen or heard part of it, or had died in the interim."*

Bill: *"How does that compare with the turn out for Norbert Phlacidly's 'view from a sparrow's armpit' that we surveyed last week?"*

Fred: *"Few down on the mother-in-laws, but we didn't get any death threats or barrages of uncontrollable laughter for mentioning this one".*

Perhaps we could simply judge in terms of which work of art you like the most. Surely we are on safe ground here – what could be simpler?

Chapter 2: The Second Not

Hmm. Like the most. In what context? To say that you like one work of art more is to, in some way, degrade the other; and as soon as we enter into any kind of gradation we are in trouble. To appreciate in its purity, without reference to anything else, surely must be the goal, albeit a tricky one to fully achieve. But then, do we not have a responsibility, as does the creator, to strive for perfection? Who said they had to do all the work?

The "like the most" measurement is blown out of the water by the introduction of a fiendish element: time. *When* do you like it the most, that favourite film of yours? When you are trying to concentrate on studying for an exam? Hardy's poems of the joys of the natural world are of little comfort when one is sunk in the depression of a dreary day. The blackness of Bosch and Beksinski's paintings, or the pessimism of Dostoyevsky just might not speak to you when you are feeling on top of the world. But at other times they may be deeply moving.

I aim to choose the music that I listen to very carefully. My collection comes from a vast array of sources and comprises almost any genre you care to mention. Yet it all has its place. Some I may listen to more than others. Can an index of value be so derived? Could we postulate that a piece of music has more value if it will be listened to more often? If it is suitable for a greater range of ambiances and occasions?

No joy here, I'm afraid. A subtle ambient piece may receive a lot of airtime from me, as it produces a perfect backdrop for a quiet evening or for when I'm studying, writing, etc. A high-powered jazz fusion album, which demands unconditional attention, may be played less frequently. But I am passionate about some of those recordings and could not be more absorbed in them when I do chose to put them on. So which is better? Neither: they are incomparable.

51

– *Time/effort consumed*

How about the length of time it took to produce the work of art, does that count for anything? Sorry, failed again. Masterpieces have been created in 15 minutes, and in 15 years. It is groundless to even argue that either a short or long period is more desirable. Some might say that a masterpiece created in five minutes is indicative of the genius of its creator. Others may accuse this of shallowness, and argue that the shear volume of energy expelled in a lifetime's toil attributes a greater worth.

Although it may at first appear easy to at least quantify this statistic, when examined further we once again run into a dead end. The reason behind this was encapsulated beautifully in an interview given to Duke Ellington, in which he was asked how long it took him to compose his classic *Mood Indigo*. "How long?" he replied, "Well, it took me 15 minutes to write it, and 25 years to learn how".

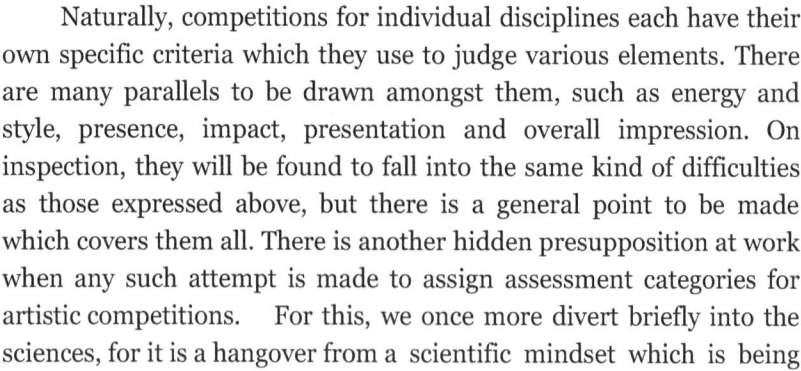

Naturally, competitions for individual disciplines each have their own specific criteria which they use to judge various elements. There are many parallels to be drawn amongst them, such as energy and style, presence, impact, presentation and overall impression. On inspection, they will be found to fall into the same kind of difficulties as those expressed above, but there is a general point to be made which covers them all. There is another hidden presupposition at work when any such attempt is made to assign assessment categories for artistic competitions.   For this, we once more divert briefly into the sciences, for it is a hangover from a scientific mindset which is being erroneously adopted for artistic analysis.

When a physicist, chemist or an engineer wants to find out about something, they are liable to break it down into its constituent parts to see what it is composed of, and how those various core elements fit together. This is perfectly valid and workable for many (but not all) subjects of physical phenomena. But art cannot be so broken down. This is the basic error. You can slice up a piece of music to unravel its harmony, rhythmic structure, orchestration, etc., but when you look into your parts bucket to find that magical quality that radiates unrestrainedly from a performance of the whole piece, you will find an empty pail. Synergy is much spoken of throughout the arts, and for good reason. If one could determine the whole by an analysis of the parts, then great art would be reducible to a simple formula. Throughout all the ages of the works of man, none has emerged, and none ever will. Oh, you can obtain certain effects by standard, well-known tricks and routines, but as anyone who has anything to do with it knows, no amount of these will combine to produce a great work of art.

Artist versus artist

Much of what has already been said is transferable to the comparison of artist to artist, or to performance versus performance, so we will cover this rapidly.

One approach is to assess technical mastery: how many paradiddles[4] a minute the drummer can play; who can draw the most perfect freehand circle, etc. But such attempts result in a sporting contest of physical dexterity to which art occasionally shows up, yawns, scratches itself, and wanders off to find something more

---

4 A basic drumming pattern consisting of four strokes, either "left, right, left, left" or "right left, right, right".

interesting to do. We may find such a competition in the field of entertainment, but they usually don't entertain for long. Furthermore, any works of art which attempt to overwhelm with technique are usually contrived and without feeling.

Technique is important. One needs to master one's tools. Studying and practising technique can make you into a skilful dancer, wordsmith, painter or illusionist, but this alone does not make you an artist. From my personal experience as a musician, I spent 10 years learning how to play fast, and 15 years trying to learn how to play slow.

We may conceivably judge the technical mastery of an artist in highly restricted constructs:

> **Premiss:** Performer A can play the Sibelius Violin Concerto.
>
> **Premiss:** Performer B cannot play the Sibelius Violin Concerto.
>
> **Conclusion:** Performer A is better than Performer B *at playing the Sibelius Violin Concerto.*

The conclusion is as much as can be deduced from this argument. But even this is not very helpful. The scenario may have arisen simply because Performer A has been practising the Sibelius Violin Concerto for the last three months, and Performer B has never encountered it. We have no indication of their overall musicianship. Performer B may be expert in Irish folk tunes and Gipsy jazz, whereas Performer A wouldn't know where to start with them. There are many facets to technical accomplishment: this painter mixes the most perfect colour, that painter inscribes the minutest of detail, the other painter produces the most realistic glass effect. One dancer performs the most pirouettes in a row, another has perfect poise and balance, another faultless timing.

We shall indulge in a slight, but worthy, digression at this point. When we see virtuoso performances and masterpiece exhibitions, it is easy to be led into thinking that this artist is capable of anything. They could paint any painting they wanted to, play any kind of music or craft any kind of sculpture. Great as they may be, this is usually not the reality. Ask Dali to paint a Monet, or vice versa, and they would have struggled. Not that they couldn't have done it, but they would have had to work at it. Dizzy Gillespie was known for dazzling Bebop trumpet gymnastics; Miles Davis for the soulful, understated melodies that seemed to flow effortlessly from his horn. For them to have mastered each other's style would have taken dedicated attention and practice.

Many schools encourage the idea of becoming a "rounded" artist; the professional should be able to turn their hand to any style when required. This may be true to a degree in picking up regular work. It is handy to have a knowledge of various genres to be able to incorporate them into one's own style. A session musician working in a studio all day recording radio jingles and TV theme tunes may have to be proficient in whatever is thrown at them. But there are only a small handful of professionals who do the vast majority of this kind of work.

The important point to note is that a lot of great artists whom we admire and are inspired by don't approach it in that fashion. They excel at *one* thing. They become known for one style – their own style. They produce such stunning examples of that style because that is what they have focused and worked upon. They haven't tried to do it all. The jacks of all are few and far between, and the aces of all are so rare as to be almost non-existent.

So there we have another good reason not to set up battle lines between artists. And here's another: have you ever witnessed a band playing where the musicians are competing against each other? Was it any good? Unlikely. The ballet falls flat on its face when everyone is trying to take the lead. The production of art, where it involves more than one person, requires a selfless spirit of cooperation. In-fighting is always detrimental, and will be evident in the final product. Solo works are not immune from this either, as the virus of one-upmanship seeps through the cracks to infect the composition with a strain of egotism.

There is a subtle, yet crucial, point to behold before we leave off this topic. It is, perhaps, more important than all that has gone before. Have you ever decided to take up sketching, gone to join a class, seen how good everyone was, and concluded that maybe it's just not for you? Ever given up on your attempts at poetry when your words didn't seem to flow as mellifluously as Wordsworth? Seen a breathtaking performance of a Paganini Concerto and thrown in the towel on your violin practice? Perhaps these things happened very early in life. Didn't make the grades in the school art class and never painted since. Big brother was ripping it out with a rock band, and you figured your meagre attempts at guitar playing would never reach that level.

This can also swing the other way. Have you ever dismissed the entirety of an artist's output because you didn't consider them good enough? Ignored a whole genre in your chosen field, because the general level of technical proficiency wasn't up to your level of competence?

The first point to make about this is a general one, covering many aspects of life, and is concisely stated in the Desiderata:

> *"If you compare yourself to others you will become vain or bitter, for always there will be greater and lesser persons than yourself."*
>
> *(Ehrmann, 1927)*

There are no masters; we are all beginners. No one is bigger than the subject. This is understood by truly great artists in any field, whether they will openly speak of it or not. They appreciate the enormity of the subject they are dealing with and become ever more cognizant of this as they progress. He who believes himself to have mastered it all is blind to the task at hand. This does not preclude one, however, from being confident of one's abilities – there is no need for self-abasement – but humbleness is desirable.

We can see that this humbleness derives not from comparison with one's contemporaries, but on reflection of one's place in the subject itself. The contest of person to person is trifling when viewed in this light. Moreover, in the context with which we are dealing in this chapter, we can spot the precise point of deviation where we went awry.

Thoughts like "I'll never be good enough to do this", "They're all so much better than me, I might as well give up", "If I can't produce work like _____, what's the point in trying?" or "they're rubbish" are all destructive. Recognise, if you find yourself harbouring any such thoughts, that *you are making art into a competition*. And it is not a competition.

Any time you fall into this trap it is time to take a step back and refocus. What did you get into this activity for in the first place? If your motivation was to beat everyone and come out on top, then perhaps you would do better to realign yourself with a sporting discipline. But if your drive is an artistic one, then make that your focus and get back to work.

Genre versus genre

"I believe that if it were left to artists to choose their own

labels, most would choose none."

(Ben Shahn)

Classifications can be useful to help us talk about or refer to different artists and their work. But the more specific one tries to become about them, which is unavoidable if some kind of ranking system is being attempted, the more they wriggle around, dance and weave, duck away from the nail with which you are trying to pin them down, and eventually seem to disappear.

Take your music collection and do this exercise as an example. Assuming you have a music collection, that is; you could just as well use a book collection, painting collection, film collection or anything of the sort. Make up a list of genres with which you are going to categorise your collection. It doesn't matter what you use – choose whatever you like, as long as it would provide some sort of sensible break down. Now take each piece in your collection, one by one, and place them into *one* and *only one* of the genres you have drawn up.

How did you get on? If you had any kind of a sizeable collection you probably had an experience of getting a few nicely pigeon-holed, then coming across one that just didn't quite seem to fit into one of the boxes you had laid out. You could maybe put it into one of them, if you squinted a bit, screwed up your face and pretended not to notice, but deep down you knew it didn't really fit there. Either that, or you came across one that could fit into two or more of the boxes. You could flip a coin, chuck it into one and be done with it. But doesn't that rankle, just a little? Doesn't seem fair, does it, to stick that label on when the work actually covers more than just that label.

You may have taken the next logical step and tried to rework your genres. "Doesn't fit into any of the boxes? Well, we'll make a new box! That showed 'em – take that!" Or you possibly tried merging two boxes together, rather than choose between them. However you did it, it doesn't really matter – the result will be the same. "Hmm, should that other one be in this new box now, or is it OK in the one I put it in? And now that I've put the funk records together with the rock records, I have James Brown slotted next to Black Sabbath – that doesn't seem right."

Keep at it – move those boxes around all you like. The more you look over your collection, the more you will notice little differences between all the items. You can't even group them under the artist that produced them, as the majority of artists will produce a range of works over their career, and don't stick to exactly the same formula for every creation. Eventually, around about the time you are thinking you either need hundreds of classifications to cover them, or one big general one for them all, the uniqueness of the works becomes apparent. "It's not a *this*, or a *that*; it just is what it is."

Art form versus art form

The battle between the arts is a futile one. Busoni argues for the superiority of music, Da Vinci puts forward a convincing case for painting over all others in his *Notes on Art and Life*. What is most interesting, however, is that they all propose the same arguments, but from opposing points of view. For example, the transient, ephemeral quality of music is laudable to Busoni, yet to Da Vinci, this very "impermanence" is an indication of its inherent inferiority.

Here's a refreshing way to look at it. Mark Applebaum, dubbed the "mad scientist of music", gave a presentation in which he described his initial training in classical piano, from which he moved on into inventing his own instruments and tonal structures. His work is highly experimental, and he found himself frequently confronted with the question "yes but, is it music?" After some deliberation, he decided to no longer entertain this question, and started instead to ask himself, "is it interesting?" Following this change of reference point he went on to produce pictorial drawings as a substitute for musical notation, pieces better described as performance art, and creations that don't easily fit into any category. He stated how moving from the identity of "Mark the musician" to adopting the identities of "Mark the artist", "Mark the inventor", "Mark the *(whatever he wanted)*" freed up his creativity to explore anything he liked, and opened up many new doors.

Art is still art, whatever form it takes. The lines of distinction are more blurred than ever in an age where multimedia productions are in the ascendency, and there is no necessity for us to consider art forms as separate entities. If the boundaries that have been erected serve only to produce squabbling, then let us dispense with the boundaries.

Summary

So we now see the *X Factor* and *Pop Idol*[5] idiocy for what it is. I'm afraid the likes of the Oscars, *Young Musician of the Year*, etc., all go the same route.

There are no winners and losers in art. This in itself may lead the way to a (descriptive) definition of art: that activity of man which cannot be reduced to sport. Most other activities can be, one way or the other. Business can be reduced to competition, as can speculating on the stock market. We compete over land, jobs, resources. We often play games in our interpersonal relationships. But art picks up its bags and leaves the moment we start to pick sides.

---

5 British TV game shows in which the contestants take part in a singing competition before a panel of judges.

To illustrate this further, consider again your Prime Experience. Were you, at the time, in a judgemental or critical frame of mind? Were you comparing that work with some other or giving them marks out of ten? This attitude itself would preclude the true experience.

Nothing in this chapter is intended to suggest that you should not work diligently at your chosen artistic endeavour, for the effort invested is valuable indeed and will repay you many times over. Yet for an artist, the only judgement he is likely to respect is that which he gives himself, and there is no harsher critic. The same can also be said of the appreciator, participator or receiver of a work of art: he will know what he got from it, or what he didn't get from it, and, if honest with himself, shall need no further evaluation. But above all, to adopt a judgemental frame of mind with regards to art is to have one's focus in completely the wrong place.

Eleven Things That Art is Not

Chapter 3

The Third *Not*

In the early part of the last century, Sigmund Freud wrote a number of papers containing his theories about the mind and human behaviour, along with an approach to therapy, and thus founded the practice of Psychoanalysis. Freud was born and raised in Austria in the latter half of the nineteenth century – a time of highly strict moral standards and accepted codes of conduct regarding personal relationships and sex. This is evident in his work, which is focused heavily upon these areas and how he believed they affected the human psyche. To Freud, neurosis was born of repressed sexual urges, which began in early childhood, and were reinforced by social mores forbidding the outlet of these desires. Granted, overbearing moral strictures can influence a person. Yet the "freedom" of values and expressions witnessed in our modern culture has done little to make man saner on the subject.

Where this ties into our current discussion is Freud's theory concerning the function of art. He believed it to be a defence mechanism which provided an alternative to the decent into neurosis via a process termed "sublimation", in which an artist is afforded a way out of his sexual repressions by channelling his fantasies into publicly acceptable artistic creations.

These ideas, not grounded in any solid evidence or proof, and contested at the time by specialists in sexual abnormalities such as Krafft Ebing and Moll, nevertheless gained acceptance and became part of Psychoanalytic doctrine. Although there have been significant advances in the study of the mind since Freud's time, which highlight the misguided nature of his assertions, these ideas still circulate widely today. We therefore need to address the area fully in our third *not*:

Art is *not* sex.

Freud dealt primarily with childhood, believing it to be the breeding ground for all later mental disturbances. Going beyond and into adult life, the theory extended the key role that repressions played in sexual abnormality and perversion to cover all areas of human activity. Most famously, the dream landscape was interpreted as phallic imagery, however he also sought to explain a widening spectrum of childhood behaviour as sexual phenomena. Not only thumb sucking and breast feeding were evidences of the child's emerging sexuality, but also the following were all sources of sexual gratification, and their actions all indicative of such desires:

- playing
- ticking
- touching/exploring body parts
- curiosities about bodies and where children come from
- itching
- muscular activity

- intellectual work
- concentration of attention
- an impulse for knowledge and investigation
- looking at cruelty
- fear of an upcoming exam
- exertion expended in the solution of a difficult task
- enjoying train rides
- wanting to be a driver or conductor

To sum up in his own words:

"If we now, in conclusion, review the evidences and indications of the sources of the infantile sexual excitement, which have been reported neither completely nor exhaustively, we may lay down the following general laws as suggested or established...

...It is possible that nothing of any considerable significance occurs in the organism that does not contribute its components to the excitement of the sexual impulse."

Equating everything to sex gives a very distorted picture – one in which all toddlers would appear as sex-crazed maniacs. A world could be conceived, through heavy blinkers, where all of man's actions were explainable as being motivated by food:

- Sex and babies – greater resources to gather food for the tribe
- Kissing – a substitute for when you are not allowed to eat something
- Business – the unconscious desire to eat one's competitors

- Dreaming – a distraction from the fact that we're not eating anything

We could explain all of our world from this viewpoint, but it wouldn't make it right. To make the point clearer, if slightly more absurd, man's activities could all be reduced to starring in TV commercials:

- Eating is just a way to gain experience with consumer goods
- We attend schools to learn about all the products we shall have to model
- Sex is simply a marketing tool, or the means to getting through an audition
- Holidays are an attempt to search the world over for the best opportunity to get in front of the camera
- Dreams are where we rehearse the future roles we shall be called upon to play

In case you hadn't spotted it, this is a trick that advertisers frequently play on us: attempting to equate all the world to their product. And consider how insane the world looks through the eyes of advertising. If it seems we are diving into the far-fetched realm of ridiculousness, then realise that G. I. Gurdjieff[6] sold hundreds of people on the idea that man's place in the cosmos exists solely as "food for the moon". He still has a strong following today.

The truth is man's actions are governed by a broad range of influences, urges and desires. The even broader range of activities he engages upon is evidence enough of this: conservation and the protection of animals, spiritual practices, intellectual pursuits, going to the match on the weekend, scientific discovery, archaeological exploration, taking a holiday in the sun or going on safari in Africa,

---

6   Armenian-born mystic, philosopher and spiritual teacher (1866-1949).

climbing a mountain, taking vitamins, getting a tattoo, helping an old lady across the road, volunteering for a charity or making a donation, to name but a few. Humans are complex beings, and they may partake of an activity simply because it interests them, or for no reason at all.

There is nothing wrong with sex, but if one were to categorise, it would have to fall into the more primitive, animalistic urges, whereas the arts appeal to the higher human senses. The connection is tenuous. Adopting the sublimation theory regarding art suggests that if everyone were sexually fulfilled, there would be no art. Or that a productive artist should be balanced and level-headed on the subject of sex and not harbour any unfulfilled desires. This doesn't fit the picture of reality that I have. If we are to accept this explanation for the urge to create art, we are also bound to draw similar conclusions for its appreciation, leading us to suppose that whenever we read a novel, attend a concert or visit a gallery, we are actually voyeurs seeking carnal satisfaction from someone publicly flaunting their sexuality. The conclusions tell us more about Freud than they do about art.

Taking a slightly different angle, yet honed on the same target, is the suggestion that art is simply a mating call akin to birdsong. There may be some parallels, as we shall presently discuss, but my primary response when I hear such citing of the animal kingdom, is to ask if the phenomena being cited has ever truly been observed. No doubt animals engage in various displays to attract a mate. Some can be quite elaborate, like the search and selection of the most attractive stone to present to the female penguin, or the highly particular "track and bowl system" created by the Kakapo[7]. Through some hopeful squint of

---

[7] The Kakapo is a rare and critically endangered species of nocturnal, flightless parrot surviving on several islands off New Zealand. They have a complex mating ritual in which the males excavate hollowed-out bowls, linked by tracks, and keep all the plants neatly clipped on either side. They will then sit in a bowl and "boom" in a deep, loud voice, all night long, to attract a female.

anthropomorphism we could even suggest some to be artistic. But I wonder if those propounding such theories have ever really listened to birds – actually stopped and taken the time to hear the variations in tone and expression, the range of intentions accompanying a variety of occasions. To attribute it all to a "mating call" is a gross over-simplification.

Whenever we hear an analysis of an animal's activity, it is invariably reduced to food or mating. These motives may well predominate the animal world, but anyone who has had a pet and observed will tell you that doesn't cover everything about them.

Red deer engage in a spectacular mating ritual, whereby the largest stags charge head-to-head in a competition of clashing antlers, snorting nostrils and pounding hooves. The victors are awarded the picking rights of all the females.

Or so it was assumed, until some people decided to observe what really went on with the whole pack of deer over a period of time. It turns out that the females are largely unimpressed by, and uninterested in, the display of overt masculinity, and slope off to have sex in the bushes with some of the younger stags while the elders bang their heads together. Whatever they are doing it for, it doesn't seem to have any actual relation to their mating habits.

If you have ever wondered whether animals create art, you may be intrigued to watch elephants painting. I first encountered this phenomenon as a child, where an elephant was observably choosing a colour from a palette, then, picking up a brush by its trunk which was loaded with said colour paint, would splash somewhat random strokes on a canvass. Amusing at the time, but little more.

There has been much development in this field since those days. As I recently discovered, elephants are now producing paintings of unmistakable skill and creativity. I'm talking of landscapes containing trees and other elephants that many people, including myself, would have been proud to produce. They even sign their own name at the end. Watching the deliberate use of technique and the concentration of these elephants at work leaves one in no doubt that they know exactly what they are doing. If you greet this information with any degree of disbelief, then I urge you to look it up – it's really quite astounding.

So are we now to suppose that elephants are sublimating their sexual urges in a socially acceptable fashion? It certainly doesn't come across that way. There are plenty of other examples of our misguided conceptions with relation to animals, and more stacking up all the time. Thus a more realistic interpretation of the "art is a mating call" hypothesis is "the attempt to superimpose an idea of an animal's activities onto the animal, then attempting to superimpose this assumed superimposition onto humans".

Taking a further step back, the science of Biology has for many years run into a brick wall when it comes to sex. There's just no acceptable way of explaining it that makes sense and fits the available evidence, from the viewpoint of genetics and evolutionary theory. It's such a frightfully inefficient method of reproduction, and so out of joint with the Darwinian concept of survival of the fittest through the preservation of the strongest genes. Decade after decade, the foremost experts in the field scratch their heads, occasionally proffering tentative theories which subsequently are shown to be inconsistent with the data of the real world, and end up conceding that they are none the wiser. The current consensus, in an attempt to cover all the puzzling anomalies that make up the big anomaly of sex, is that it must be an amalgamation of reasons why nature has settled upon this seemingly unprofitable course, but we don't know what they all are.

Given that our current theories on the laws of nature have no way of explaining anything fundamental about the subject of sex, it is difficult to see how we could assert a thorough understanding of the mechanisms by which art manifests itself in human activities as a direct result of sex. This would surely be trying to run before we had evolved legs.

So do we extricate sex from art altogether? Unfortunately, that would be difficult. There is a video doing the rounds entitled "Music is not a meritocracy", wherein two YouTube videos were held up as examples, one featuring a blind, young Japanese lad performing with spectacular expertise on an electric guitar, the other of a girl playing an acoustic guitar. The girl is very attractive and showing a generous amount of cleavage, and her video outnumbers the amount of views obtained on the young lad's video by a ratio of 40:1. The inference being made was that ugly bands are never going to make it big, and "it's like your parents told you: life isn't fair, get used to it".

The composer and bassist Adam Neely tempered this hotly-delivered argument, highlighting the important point being made was that whereas there may not be a meritocracy, there is something to be said for the way a work is presented. He cited the French avant-garde musical movement *Music Concrète,* who would play taped recordings to a live audience with nothing but loud speakers on the stage, and noted that the audiences which attended this kind of show were unsurprisingly small. Presentation does make a difference. The impression and impact of a painting will be effected by the lighting, space and ambience of the room in which it is hung. These are both valid points of view, and we can help to clean up some of the space between without disturbing either one of them.

The Classical pianist Yuja Wang has gained a reputation for her sensational virtuosity, and is currently one of the most sought-after musicians in the world. She has also gained a reputation for the exotic, and often revealing, dresses in which she chooses to perform. This last divides opinion, and sadly takes up more column inches in comments and reviews than the first. The battle lines form between those protesting that she shouldn't be allowed wear such attire and accusing her of looking like a lady of ill repute, and those proclaiming her rights as a modern, powerful woman, asserting she can wear what she likes and shouldn't have to put up with lecherous men making derogatory comments. There is, of course, the third group of those just making the lecherous comments.

These, often bitterly spoken viewpoints, are not quite getting to the heart of the matter, which is that the discussions about the dresses are taking all the attention, and not the music. Personally, I think she looks great and I would defend her right to dress as she pleases, the same as I would for anyone. This, however, does not absolve one from all consideration of what is appropriate. You wouldn't wear Bermuda shorts to a funeral, or a bikini to your job at the bank. But even here we are getting slightly off track; social acceptability is a minor issue. I would ask Ms. Wang what she wanted to achieve with her art. She is evidently passionate about the music that she plays, and is surely intelligent enough to be fully aware of the effects that she creates. The choice is hers, and she has the power to decide where the focus is placed and how she wishes to inspire her audiences.

Yuja Wang is not the only example, as others are following suit, no doubt drawn to the publicity and attention, or encouraged to embrace it by their managers. Understandable, in that it can be a tough world to make your way in. Plus, after all, it's nice to make the most of one's opportunities and the doors they may open.

While on the subject of auxiliary benefits, there is another aspect to consider. Although primarily being a competitive discipline, there are no doubt extraneous benefits to partaking in sport – to keep fit, impress members of the opposite sex, etc. Just as such, there may be auxiliary motives for engaging in an "artistic" pursuit – for some, attraction of the opposite sex. But such motives are not likely to drive one to the selfless dedication needed to truly master that craft. Perhaps there is value in the additional bonuses of both sport and artistic pursuit, but in neither case are they a substitute for, nor should they be confused with, the core theme.

There is nothing wrong with feeling an attraction for someone. Although, an infatuation for someone you've never met and are never likely to meet (which the multimedia pop culture fosters) is probably not healthy. But admiration is fine, and you are not evil for feeling a sexual attraction toward someone. No doubt a great entertainer or artist may attract this kind of attention – it is only natural. But the sexual attraction is not the art. It may be a secondary reaction to an artful experience, but it is not the same thing.

Consider again your Prime Experience – was it a sexual urge? Such feelings may have entered as a side effect, but it is not likely to have been at the core of the experience. The industries which have built up around the arts will all try to use the same promotional tools as marketing divisions and advertising companies use for all manner of businesses. Sex sells, it may be true, but it is trivial by comparison to the potential power of art. This will not stop Hollywood from portraying film stars as perfect physical specimens, pop videos from using sex appeal in place of artistic talent, and theatre shows from covering their posters and merchandise in provocative imagery.

We could point out, however, that we are not examining anything new. The nude has been a favourite topic of painting for centuries, with these only gaining their inspiration from the naked sculptures of Greece, stretching back over millennia. We would have to concede artistic value in at least some of these works, so perhaps the poignant question revolves around the boundary, should we assume there to be one, between art and pornography.

Firstly, I would liken this issue to bad taste in jokes or offensive humour – the question of what is acceptable and what oversteps the mark. Vetoing particular topics is highly subjective, so I believe a useful approach is to focus on the intention. If the aim behind the deliverance was to make someone laugh, to amuse, to entertain and provide relief, then so be it – fair game. If the aim was to be nasty, hurtful or simply crude, then it should meet disapproval. It is usually clear, to anyone openly paying attention, which category it falls into. And so it is with aesthetic or salacious intentions in works of art.

What may confuse the issue is the sexual deviant, with a distorted fixation on the subject. He or she may be incapable of looking upon the image of a naked body without sexual connotation, whereas a sane mind can find beauty in it. We need to recognise that such conditions exist and separate out, where possible, the aberration from the appreciation of art.

This returns us to Freud, highlighting another narrowed lens he was peeping through: Freud was studying abnormality. He had a lifetime of dealing with mentally unstable patients, examining their neuroses and psychoses (with which he made, quite notably, little progress in curing) and concocting theories to explain it all away. Looking only to aberrated, malfunctioning examples in order to draw general conclusions produces a much distorted picture. If one were to exclusively study collapsed bridges, demolished buildings and rusted, disused machinery, one would get a pretty obscure concept of engineering.

Yet it is such a distorted view which has given rise to the idea that people are somehow propelled into great achievement by their mental instability; as if a touch of insanity were an asset, or even a prerequisite to a career of ingenuity and brilliance. But if we wish to know from where the excellence came, we have to study the excellence of the being. We need to understand their abilities, not their disabilities.

The idea that genius equals madness, the notion of "be glad you're neurotic", is a nonsense. People are hampered by their mental aberrations, not helped by them. Who knows what wonders van Gogh would have turned out, and over a longer period, had he not frequented the asylum. We can only speculate what such minds would have produced had they been free to unleash their creative power to full capacity. The best musicians and artists I have been fortunate enough to encounter, people at the top of their profession, have in the main been the sanest, nicest people you could wish to meet. That's how they managed to get there.

The insidious claim that great artists are madmen has influenced generations of budding artists, encouraged by the media, that they should be a bit crazy, "off the rails", go wild. The "eccentricity" of the artist is a cliché. Nothing is further from the truth. That a few individuals have risen to great heights in spite of their debilitating afflictions is no evidence that the afflictions in any way aided them. You don't need to try and be "an artist". You don't have to be anything other than what you are.

This chapter could therefore not only be predicated upon the statement "art is *not* sex", but also "art is *not* a disorder". At its finest, it is the pinnacle of human achievement.

Chapter 4

The Fourth *Not*

We shall revisit the subject of semantics for a moment to complete an unfinished tale. Focusing on the idea that words are subject to producing generalisations, distortions and associations, and the implications which follow therefrom, some twentieth-century thinkers have drawn startling conclusions. There are those who suggest that all language is therefore misleading, inevitably forming a barrier to communication, or profess that "language is a lie". Extrapolations have even been voiced that ultimately no communication of any kind is possible.

Nice theory, but the proof of the pudding is that when I talk to someone they generally understand what I mean. The theories seem to have gotten lost somewhere away from our common experience. It is interesting to note that those putting forward such ideas use language to explain how useless language is, in a similar vein to the philosophers who use reason to explain how reason can't explain anything.

It may be true that language is an abstraction of reality – a representative model of our subjective experience of a part of reality. But the thing to understand, and the point that Korzybski was trying to make, is that this is only a problem if we take language, or any other map we are using, to be reality itself. It is easy to see how confusions and conflicts will arise if we take tiny, selective simplifications and assume them to be a literal picture of the whole. Once we appreciate that they are merely abstractions which help us to conceptualise and convey ideas, then language, symbols, models and maps actually become very useful.

Language, then, is just one of many methods for transmitting a communication. Sometimes it may work well, but in other circumstances it may be more efficacious to use another method. The pictograms of Traditional Chinese writing blur the distinction between pictures and words, and leads us into the idea of using imagery for communication. Music is often referred to as a language. I'm sure you can see where this is going.

There is no doubt that ideas, emotions, concepts, realities, logics, aesthetics and many other things are conveyed through art forms. It is a most powerful method of achieving this. There are often distinguishable originators and receipt points for artistic creations, giving the appearance of a cause-effect relationship. Among its many facets, art has the power of communication.

This is so much the case, that some have been tempted to equate art to communication, and to explain all its manifestations from this point of reference. To quote:

> *"All art is communication of the artists' ideas, sounds, thoughts; without that no one will support the artist."*
>
> *(Lionel Hampton)*

Chapter 4: The Fourth Not

> *"Art is a means of communication by which mind reaches out to mind across great gaps of space and time, as well as across death."*
>
> *(Francis Hoyland)*

> *"Art is essentially communication. It doesn't exist in a vacuum. That's why people make art, so other people can relate to it."*
>
> *(Conor Oberst)*

But here we reach our next *not*:

Art is *not* communication.

Note that we are not suggesting that art cannot be communicative, but that it is not synonymous with communication. As hinted at above, there are many facets to art, and we will fail to see the elephant in the room if we clutch only at its tail. To illustrate:

Question: *What is a tree?*

Answer: *It's green.*

This answer is not incorrect; most trees are, indeed, green. But does that describe what one *is*? Does it encompass the understanding that you have of trees? Their functions, physical make-ups, life processes, varieties, roles in the ecosystem? Clearly, "It's green" could only be called a definition of a tree in the very loosest and virtually useless sense of the word.

Hardly needing to be pointed out, a first path of inquiry into this proposed definition may see one hold up an apple or blade of grass and ask: "Are these, then, trees?" How many green objects are there in the environment? In this way we see that, although trees may be green, it doesn't really help us as a definition.

Words flow between people. Radio signals transmit across the airwaves. Birdsong twitters in the trees. Satellite TV broadcasts to the millions. We have radar, sonar, telephone lines, mobiles, wireless, base stations, video calls, all crackling through the skies. There's light signals, smoke signals, blazing beacons atop of hills, well-oriented carrier pigeons, less well-oriented postmen. Just how many kinds of communication are there in our environment?

We can take this a stage further. When viewed through a particular lens, what is there that could not be reduced to or described by communication? A war is a type of communication. A brush on the cheek with a feather is a communication. To ignore someone or "give them the cold shoulder" is a communication. You can communicate with the floor by jumping on it. When you paint a wall you are communicating with the wall, and the paint, and the brush. A surfer communicates with the waves, as does a footballer with a ball and an archer with his bow 'n' arrows (along with anything he hits).

Therefore, to say that art is communication is to not say anything at all. One might as well say "art is everything". It is the kind of definition which arises when trying to encompass too many elements under the same umbrella. Any concise description which attempts to cover a Chopin piano concerto and the *Birdie Song* in the same breath will perforce be too broad to be meaningful.

To argue that art reflects the *quality* of communication is not much of an improvement, and disappears down logical black holes at every turn. What is meant by "quality"? If we try to define *that* slippery character we find ourselves just chasing synonyms, as was more than adequately covered by Robert Pirsig in *Zen and the Art of Motorcycle Maintenance*.

If one were to suggest that we mean an *accurate* communication, then I would ask one to consider a well directed punch on the nose. It certainly leaves the recipient in no doubt about the intended communication. But regardless of the degree of skill with which it were delivered, or the degree of emotional response it elicited, if one were to suggest that a punch on the nose were a work of art I would suggest that we were talking different subjects.

To see where we have gone astray, it is important to understand that a perfect communication may completely miss the mark as a work of art. A road sign may emphatically convey its message. It may be important and extremely relevant to the driver, and he may have gained some understanding as a result. He may even feel an extreme emotional response. It ticks all the boxes of a high quality communication, but it is not art.

The basic aim of a communication is to take an idea from one place and to put it somewhere else. The road sign can be considered an excellent communication if the situation that it was warning about was transferred directly to the driver's head, so that he understood exactly what the person who made the sign wanted him to understand. "STOP". It's very clear, and we don't want any deviations, embellishments or distortions. The driver got the message, and he stopped.

When we come to a work of art, however, we do not seek a total and utter replication in the mind of the recipient. For starters, getting a communication across perfectly presupposes the ability of the recipient to receive that communication, which they may not possess, due to many possible factors such as education or plain willingness.

But art transcends such considerations – we are not concerned by them.

Then there is the issue of perception. If we take the same tree spoken of above, I may say it is green and you may also say that it is green. But we have no way of telling that what you call green and what I call green are the same thing. We may look at Van Gogh's *Starry Night* and marvel at the expressiveness of his swirling lines and wonder how he arrived at using such an effect. For all we know, he may have been trying to paint exactly what he saw. Perhaps the world looked precisely like that to him. We shall never know if we perceive things the same way as the artist.

This state of affairs may be seen as a barrier to communication, but when it comes to art *it doesn't matter*. The poet and the playwright will deliberately choose ambiguous words and phrases. The painter may only hint at forms, so too the sculptor and even the architect. A piece of performance art or contemporary dance will leave itself open to a multitude of interpretations. The artist embraces the vague and indistinct, and avoids the literal. It matters not whether we can precisely decipher their exact thought. In fact, we may say that it is a requisite component of art that we do not – a theme we shall return to later. We don't utilise the power of art by stamping in a message with a branding iron.

To enter a qualifier like "quality" into the equation is also suggestive of a sliding scale of art; some yardstick with which to measure the "artfulness" of an object or phenomenon. "This book is more arty than that one". Such concepts have already been dealt with under "art is not a competition". Of course, it is natural to compare things. As humans, we do it all the time, and it is a primary mechanism behind understanding. Should we even wish to, it would be virtually impossible to stop ourselves comparing art works with others. But this comparison need only be in terms of differences and similarities – the means through which understanding is achieved. We don't have to enter into value judgements.

Another commonly proposed refinement is to reduce the definition of art to "a communication of beauty". For some, this is purely a subjective matter – Shakespeare's immortal phrase "Beauty lies in the eye of the beholder" springs to mind. Concepts in philosophy often come around full circle, as they do in fashions, and we see this viewpoint supported by the Existentialists, who would claim that the only meaning to be had in anything is that which is imbued by the individual. Although limited, it is at least more positive than its forerunner: the Nihilistic doctrine of "there is no meaning to anything".

To explain its limitations, let us first assume the assertion to be true, that the conception of beauty is purely a subjective matter, and that one's personal opinion is all that counts. We would then have to accept the psychopath's belief that slitting a victim's throat and watching the blood poor out is beautiful. I would rather suggest that he is mentally ill.

Without wishing to dive into a tiresome list of similar examples, let us cut to the chase. We now have an individual, bright eyed and beaming with joy, enthusiastically claiming that the sculpture in front of her is exquisitely beautiful. However, no sculpture lies before her – just an empty space. The beauty exists wholly in her mind, and if she believes that she sees it in front of her, then who are we to question her totally subjective viewpoint?

The obvious difficulty with this is that without any sculpture being present, nothing has actually been communicated. This puts pay to our idea of art being a communication of beauty. Moreover, we have thrown an imponderable over the purely subjective nature of the appreciation of beauty, for we have highlighted a paradox to which

81

such ideas of subjectivity inevitably lead.

Our example of an omitted sculpture provides a picture of the ultimate subjective position. But this is not only the ultimate, for were we to introduce any sculpture at all for consideration we would be providing an object. If we concede that the viewer sees the sculpture, then a communication has taken place, and the object has therefore contributed in some degree to the subject's opinion. When we talk of a work of art as existing anywhere outside of a person's mind, we cannot consider its appreciation to be a purely subjective matter. Thus we could introduce an additional *not* which puts pay to an old, and at times frustrating, idea: art is *not* just whatever you like.

Nor, by a similar line of reasoning, can we consider it purely objective. And this matches our experience of the world, as it is clear that people do indeed have differing appreciations of the same works of art. We could propose a number of reasons behind the disparity of opinions, one being the cultural background of the individual, or their degree of familiarity with that which has been presented to them. For example, I once read a tale of pioneers who contacted a remote village in Africa. One was an accomplished artist, in the European tradition, and had made a gift to the tribal elders of one of his paintings, which depicted one of his fellow travellers riding a horse. The villagers, unaccustomed to seeing western art, stared at the picture in bemusement, utterly unable to make out what it was supposed to be.

We could, therefore, adopt the model that a combination of both the beholder and the beheld contribute to a realisation of beauty. We needn't, however, delve any more deeply into subjective/objective dichotomy, as it should be clear by now that it will provide us with no elucidation. Besides, what we have been discussing, the expression and perception of beauty, is actually the field of aesthetics – a closely related, but not identical, topic to art. Aesthetics has been a keenly debated branch of philosophy for as far back as anybody can remember. Many strains of the subjective/objective question have featured throughout the ages without sign of any resolution, accompanied by the shifting from side to side of what are essentially re-phrasings of the same old themes. All very suggestive that we don't really understand the question that we are asking. It just doesn't make sense to think in these terms, to create this arbitrary division. As we shall see later, there are other ways of approaching the issue.

Back to focusing on art, rather than simply aesthetics, another question arises with regard to the topic of this chapter: is it possible to have art without communication? This has the flavour of a parallel with the classic Zen koan[8]: If a work of art appears in a wood, but there is no-one around to perceive it, is it art? This is difficult to address without doing a U-turn back down the road of the subject/object dichotomy, but pondered for long enough, as with its Zen koan counterpart, one would hopefully transcend this restrictive frame of reference to reach a higher plateau of thought. We shall leave the deep ponderings for another time and look at a factor which may lead to a simpler solution.

If you are an artist, for whom do you create art? Aside from pieces that may be produced for or dedicated to specific persons, what is the impetus behind your creations? Many artists produce works of art simply because they want to create them, without necessarily showing them to anyone. It is usually only the non-artist who believes that the audience provides the motivation. This may be the case for an entertainer, but the artist seldom relies on an external source as a target to aim towards. This point was captured by David Walker:

---

8   Zen koans are succinct, often paradoxical, questions, statements or stories which are used as an aid to meditation, with the aim of breaking down the confines of the usual modes of thought and reliance upon reason, and hopefully thereby attaining intuitive enlightenment or insights into life and the world. The koan being referred to and imitated in the above passage is: "if a tree falls in a forest and no-one is around to hear it, does it make a sound?"

> "I believe that the making of art is primarily for the benefit of the artist. If what the artist has created communicates messages and feelings to others, then it is because of the universality of the human experience that is speaking through the work of art."

The artist may, quite justifiably, consider the work he has created to be art before it has been shared with anyone. The communication of that which he has produced may also be a significant event, but it was nonetheless art prior to this event. We could argue that the artist is communicating to himself, but we would be both splitting hairs and condemning ourselves to encircling a self-referential no-mans-land. Besides, the pursuit of art is liberating, whereas too much talking to oneself is the road to madness.

So we have taken a brief look at whether art can exist outside of communication, now we turn to the question of whether there are elements of art that go *beyond* communication. William Golding, for one, would argue that there are:

> "Art is partly communication, but only partly. The rest is discovery"

An interesting statement, for sure, which spawns a host of other questions. What is discovered? How does this come about? What *else* is there that art does? You may have some answers, having examined your Prime Experience. Tantalising as this might be, however, we first have a few more *nots* to attack.

Chapter 5

The Fifth *Not*

The artist *Squarepusher* is most well known for producing solo albums of a highly energetic blend of frantic drum 'n' bass, powerful jazz fusion, and all manner of other (often super speedy) electronic sources. As an instrumentalist he is primarily an electric bass player, and a skilful one at that. I came across a video on YouTube featuring him in the unfamiliar setting of a live performance of solo bass guitar. The music was subtle, melodic, and I was enjoying it, when I noticed the following comment that had been submitted under the video:

> "He needs to stick to pushing squares. Yea, he's good, but he's trying to do something that prodigious jazz musicians do. And he's just...eh...not there, So come on haters. Bring it on. I'll post up some videos of me playing exactly the same stuff. And I'm A GUTARIST by trade. He's not there."
>
> *(Brian Press)*

Any skilful musician is capable of playing a sizeable repertoire. Does this mean that he shouldn't listen to any of that music? Or that it isn't any good? An artist may possess the technical proficiency to reproduce a Degas, Picasso, or certainly a Mondrian. Does this fact negate his appreciation of those works? That a thousand others could replicate a work makes no less of that work. A polite, yet firm response to this above comment may be surmised as: "Thank you for your opinion. No one is interested in your ego; we are interested in music".

The comparison to his own abilities, however, has already been covered in the chapter on *Art is not a competition*. We are here viewing from another angle. Mr. Press has made a common error in his appraisal of the video which was provided for him; an error which exemplifies our fifth *not*:

Art is *not* an individual.

The curious aspect to note about the quote above is that it makes no reference to the music being performed, only to the performer. To put into perspective just how odd this attitude is, let us consider some examples. If you had attended a university and spent all of your lectures assessing how good you thought the professor was at public speaking, how much do you think you would have learned? When at the cinema, do you bother yourself about the proficiency of the projectionist?

Such a misplaced focus can swing both ways. We can broaden the elicitation of sexual attention, spoken of in chapter 3, to say that if you are trying to make yourself interesting, and believe that this makes you an artist, you are missing the point. Ego plays no part in art. It is not about the person, but about the art itself.

The cult of the celebrity has given us countless scores of camera-

Chapter 5: The Fifth Not

hogging wannabes, trying to be famous for being famous. Fame, by itself, is not a contribution to the world. The lack of substance inherent in such empty ambitions gives rise to phrases like "My life is my art". No, I'm afraid your life is your life. It is the thing that happens between you being born and you dying, whether you want it to or not. If you wish to introduce some art into the world during that period then you are going to have to do some work.

The fact that you are alive and have a personality is something to be grateful for, but not something that makes you special or deserving of attention. There are over seven billion people on the planet, all with personalities and all with the same basic human rights. It is what you *do*, what you can create, that can be important.

Naturally, the art world will never be immune to flashes of egotism. In some cases it can be more endearing than nauseous. Salvador Dali once said that you need two things to be a great painter: 1) to come from Spain, and 2) to be called Salvador Dali. But he had something to back it up with – the guy could paint. Charismatic characters can be very entertaining, but to get caught up in all the antics is to be dazzled by the street lights and miss the stars. Unfortunately, many appear determined to be so dazzled.

At the extreme end of this behaviour, the idol worship is painful to behold: the screaming crowds that would raise alarm in any other quarter; the surrounding oneself with every scrap of merchandise and paraphernalia that the credit card will stretch to; the crying pitiful tears of hopeless adoration, destined never to be returned. One wonders what purpose is served by these acts of self-abnegation. We have no need to go to extremes, however, as the milder strains of studying biographies can be just as puzzling. They may be great individuals, but the focus should be on their artwork. That is what they wanted you to have. That is what they ploughed their life into and what you can benefit from. The day-to-day details of their workaday lives, family issues, money problems, upbringing, romances, etc., are of no more significance or importance than anyone else's. They are just the consequences of having to exist on planet Earth. Personally, I have no desire to read someone's diary, follow them around, peep over their shoulder, eavesdrop on their conversations. That could get you arrested for stalking. Why should the hounding and exposure of public figures, dead or alive, be tolerated? I may be a passionate fan of an artist's work, but I'm not the least interested in what they had for breakfast. And I respect their privacy.

In his excellent book *Amusing Ourselves to Death*, Neil Postman charts the effects of moving from a literary culture to a primarily visual one. Written over thirty years ago, his words are becoming ever more poignant in the modern day, where books are increasingly being discarded in favour of Instant-Messaging[9]. We have become so indoctrinated into the push-button ideology of instant gratification, that fewer and fewer people are seeking out or producing anything of real substance. With our insistences on "being social" we flitter away the hours in frivolities as we usher in the *Brave New World*[10] of entertainment saturation.

Why so many people are eager to wash their laundry in public is a curious question. Yet a still more baffling one is why anybody would want to watch them. As the world dives deeper and deeper into superficiality, there are times when I feel embarrassed for us as a species. We are in possession of technology that unites the entire globe with communication lines, and collects the near totality of the

---

9 An online form of chat in which messages, often very brief (perhaps only a couple of words, abbreviations or even symbolic icons), are exchanged between two or more parties over a network.
10 A dystopian novel written by Aldous Huxley in 1936, imagining a futuristic totalitarian regime in which the population are "happily" kept under control by drugs, hypnotic command, and an abundance of entertainment sources to keep them amused. Most remain unaware of, and indeed ask for, their suppression.

Chapter 5: The Fifth Not

accumulated knowledge of the race for us at the touch of a button. To see the utter pointless trivialities that we use it for the majority of the time should make us hang our heads in shame. And I mean the majority of the time – gormlessly gawping into smartphones, regardless of circumstance. Were we to be contacted by an alien race, I'm sure they would have difficulty comprehending the banality of it all.

Hopefully we are simply going through a teething phase. We have not previously had the ability for individuals to communicate globally as we do today, and our usage of this privilege is reminiscent of a child with a new toy – throwing it around, trying to eat it, hitting things with it and dropping it in muddy puddles. Perhaps we shall begin to mature and realise that the Birthday present we were given was a shiny new tool kit and we can do something more constructive with it.

It's time to get more selective about what we want to express to the world. We are drowning in content but suffocating in it's shallowness. Talk is cheap because supply exceeds demand. Andy Warhol once said "The idea is not to live forever, it is to create something that will." It's difficult to see how much, if any, of our current "social media" waffle will have any significance in a hundred years, or even ten. How many of the details of your daily life will hold any sway a century from now? That should give you an idea how much use it is to anyone in the present. If you were to produce something that was looked upon with serious consideration many years into the future, what would you want that something to be? What would you like to contribute to the forward progress of the human race?

A work of art should not be offered to the world in the hope of self-adoration. A true artist needs no praise; neither do they seek it. They know in themselves whether they are producing what they want. When one is fortunate enough to meet a great artist, one is usually struck by their humility.

Not that we should wish to make artists into bland automatons, mechanically going through the motions. Individuality is celebrated in the arts and it can be expressed to the fullest. But overt displays of attention seeking are not welcome – save them for the press conferences. There are bigger goals to target.

A helpful piece of advice arises. If you are giving a performance and you find your attention being directed inwardly, or if the eyes upon you are penetrating through your self-consciousness, making you wonder how you are coming across to people, then decide to direct your attention back onto the art, and your audience is bound to follow. And everyone will have a better time. Granted, this can be easier said than done, but with practice it can become a healthy habit. It is not limited to public performances, but has applicability during any artistic endeavour.

Your art needs to shine through you. Don't let yourself get in the way.

Chapter 6

The Sixth *Not*

In 1550, Giorgio Vasari provided the Duke of Florence with the first edition of his *Lives of the Most Eminent Painters, Sculptors and Architects* – a comprehensive work spanning ten volumes. Along with detailing their lives, Vasari inevitably discusses the artist's work, providing critiques and making mention of many pieces that he refers to by content, location or other features, but curiously not by their titles. This is because, back in those days, they didn't have any.

The convention through the classical music era was for composers to simply number their pieces for reference. Even famous titles like Da Vinci's *Mona Lisa* and Beethoven's *Moonlight Sonata* were not called such by their creators – the names were added later by others. In fact, the naming of art works is a distinctly modern practice. It is not clear exactly when and where it originated. Up to the present day it is still common for gallery owners, curators, critics or patrons to name a piece rather than the artist.

Looking for possible causes behind this development, we get a clue from the treatment of Whistler's most famous painting *Whistler's Mother*. At least, that's what it has come to be called. In 1871 it was nearly rejected for exhibition at the London Royal Academy of Art when it was submitted under its original title of "Arrangement in Grey and Black". The public and the Academy members wanted a more descriptive title, so Whistler was forced to subtitle the piece "Portrait of the Artist's Mother" for the exhibition. It is from this that the commonly-known title is derived.

One has to ask, is a name really necessary? If an artist painted a cat, it would seem pointless to call the painting "Cat". A literal, more descriptive title like "Picture of a Small Black and White Cat Looking Slightly to the Left That I Painted Last Thursday" wouldn't offer much improvement. If anything, it would detract from the experience. Naming it "Spiral Dawn Blown from the Sneeze of a Tulip" would be similarly pointless. Whistler himself expressed his bafflement over the "Arrangement in Grey and Black" affair when writing in 1890: "To me it is interesting as a picture of my mother; but what can or ought the public to care about the identity of the portrait?"

Yet is seems that it holds great importance for some. I recently attended an exhibition and was intrigued to observe a woman scurrying around the rooms, exclusively looking at all the name tags and descriptions alongside the pieces. The paintings themselves scarcely received a passing glance. At least this is a step up from the brigade of happy snappers who are incapable of looking at anything if it isn't through an iPhone, yet the woman is not alone in her behaviour. We frequently see bands of followers traipsing round a gallery or museum, avidly watching and listening to the tour guide in preference to what might be on display. Programs and long-winded explanations commonly attract more attention than the pieces they attempt to describe. The viewing room may be empty, but the visitors surround the videoed interview with the artist like bees to a honeypot.

When asked why they take interest in such things, people often answer with misgivings about not understanding the work unless they know the title and something about it.

What causes people to feel like this? It's tempting to toy with ideas of the "estrangement of art from the common people" or the "mystique created and propounded by the art world", but there is a more deeply-rooted core to unearth. So before entertaining the notion that it is a perfectly natural response, let's rephrase the question more specifically: what leads a person to believe that reading words that someone else has written, or listening to someone talk about a painting, would be more beneficial, more informative, more interesting or more important than simply *looking* at the painting for themselves? After all, artists have repeatedly spoken of the futility of talking about art:

> *"Whatever is valuable in painting is precisely what one is incapable of talking about."*
>
> *(George Braque)*

> *"People who try to explain pictures are usually barking up the wrong tree."*
>
> *(Pablo Picasso)*

> *"If you can talk about it, why paint it?"*

> *"It's always hopeless to talk about painting – one never does anything but talk around it."*
>
> *(Francis Bacon)*

Eleven Things That Art is Not

> *"An artist cannot speak about his art any more than a plant can discuss horticulture."*
>
> *(Jean Cocteau)*

If you feel the need to write a great monologue to explain the origin, meaning and import of your painting, then perhaps consider whether you are producing a work of art or writing a thesis. A work of art should stand alone; it requires no explanation. Besides, you are dealing with a higher medium than language when you are dealing with art. Why subordinate art so? Does the Mona Lisa need a speech bubble?

The issue is not restricted to painting:

> *"Until the 20th century it was generally assumed that a writer had said what he had to say in his works."*
>
> *(John Updike)*

A piece of pure music is purely abstract. It is a strange concept to suggest that one *could* offer a verbal interpretation of its meaning. *That* is the nonsensical part. It is surely more confusing to add a name to an assemblage of notes, and serves only to restrict the work to a representation of a particular thing, whereas it previously enjoyed the freedom of abstract potentiality. We're taking Magritte's *Treachery of Images*[11] a stage further if we are to imagine that a collection of sounds equates to a discourse.

Unfortunately, this practice is promoted by arts councils, colleges and charitable foundations which provide funding for projects based

---

11 A painting by surrealist artist Rene Margitte, depicting a pipe, with the words *"Ceci n'est pas une pipe"* (This is not a pipe) written below it.

on long-winded descriptions of the themes and motives of the proposed work. These difficulties are largely a product of living in a money-based society. Without going into this any further, as it would be heading into a different book, just consider that we have not always had a money-based society, and we may not always have one in the future. There are alternatives, and the world is changing fast.

So the shrouding of art works in explanatory texts has as its possible origins the craving for clarification from patrons, gallery owners and the public, plus the encouragement to provide such adornments from funding and educative organisations. The artists themselves, however, are not absolved from responsibility. One may construe an insistence on providing "contextual data" and "background" as an admission by the artist of their failure to express what they wanted through their work. In the words of Anthony Caro: "Let the work speak for itself".

As a natural consequence, the activities of art critics, music journalists and their like are brought into question. Paintings are to be looked at, not verbally interpreted; music is to be listened to, not written about; a play is to be watched, not critiqued. Art is to be experienced, as food is to be eaten and clothes to be worn. This stance is generally regarded as "L'art pour l'art" or "art for art's sake" – a purist's phrase which dates back to somewhere in the early 1800s, but which brings forward with it the inappropriate connotation that art serves no utilitarian purpose, merely an aesthetic one. This is a grave mistake.

The appeal for art to be "independent of all claptrap" was largely an attempt to distance it from the didactic role set by the state or official religion, which had a domineering influence up to that time. Over the last couple of centuries, as various regimes increasingly sought to employ art as a propaganda tool, so too have people increasingly sought to use it to expose, react to and protest against those same regimes, in what has come to be collectively known as "Political Art".

Social commentary is vitally important. Political ideas and ideals need to be communicated, prejudices and injustices challenged, and voices given to those who have been denied them. There are many media by which this can be done, and it can often be made all the more powerful through provocative imagery, compelling music and rousing prose. From Shostakovich's back-handed swipe at Stalin, through to the overt protestations of the *Guerrilla Girls*[12], the last hundred years or so in particular has seen ever more outlets for highlighting racial issues, the plight of minority groups, and so forth.

It is not difficult to see how these developments have also been a contributing factor to the tendency for verbose explanations of what a work of art "really means". If you are trying to convey a message, especially one that you feel passionate about, then you want to make sure that it gets across. Ambiguity, in this case, presents a barrier that a literal interpretation can help to break down.

Yet, as was mentioned earlier in the book, we may not be seeking literalness in art. And, as was covered earlier in this chapter, there is a difficulty with the verbal explanations. So, how to resolve these apparent conflicts? This is where we come to examine the commonality between the strains that led to the descriptive embellishments of an artistic work, and where we can derive our sixth *not:*

Art is *not* a statement.

Let's be clear, I seek to censor no-one. It would be quite

---

12 A group formed in New York in 1985 by female activists hoping to highlight issues of sexism and racism in the art community. They wear gorilla masks in public to maintain anonymity.

ridiculous to suggest that we should take the whole edifice of "Political Art" and throw it in the bin. One would need to be particularly blind, deaf and stupid to believe that it all had no value, worth or purpose. We could, however, benefit from defining that worth and purpose.

The group *Political Art Documentation and Distribution* (PAD/D) sprang up in New York in the 1980's. The group's mandate was "to provide artists with an organized relationship to society, to demonstrate the political effectiveness of image making, and to provide a framework within which progressive artists can discuss and develop alternatives to the mainstream art system." And herein lies the problem. No doubt the organisation was well intentioned, but these are three completely separate issues that head in different directions, and none of them are helped by confusing one with another.

The "political effectiveness of image making" is apparent. It can be extremely powerful, whether we refer to photography, illustration, collage, or any other kind of imagery. Yet there is no need to stop at imagery. We could speak of drama, music, or any other medium. They are all effective forms of communication when used for that purpose.

If one made a political statement in a speech, it would be regarded as nothing more than a political speech. If, however, one decided to make the same statement in a poem, it is deemed to be art. Why is the speech not art? Why do some media acquire the label of "art" and others not? In this sense, they are all simply forms of communication. If we were to suppose that art is media other than the spoken or written word, then what of semaphore, sign language, Morse code and smoke signals? Why do we not commonly consider these to be artistic?

This is an indication, along with the fact that it would be impossible to define a boundary of what constitutes "political art", that we are using unsuitable means for dividing these things up. Here again, we have cause to distance the idea that "all painting is art" or "all music is art". If you are finding that you need to provide exhaustive explanations or long-winded titles to describe the meaning of your work, then the communication you are putting forward *is* the explanation or title. The imagery or other media is merely an appendage – the use of an alternative media to add impact to the message.

A political statement is just that: a political statement. The medium which is used to make that statement is largely irrelevant. You choose the one that will best get the job done and get the message across. This is the direct communication spoken of in Chapter 4, and it serves a quite obvious and undeniable purpose.

Does this mean that an artist should not engage in political commentary? Of course not. The artist is free to pass political comment in the same way that everyone in the society should be, and he can choose any medium he likes to do so. The artist, however, in his role as an artist, has a more important function to fulfil.

Then where are we to look for a purpose in art if it not be to make political statements and social commentary? What should be the artist's "organised relationship to society"? He is not a politician. Nor is he a philosopher. He can influence those fields, but it is not his primary function.

For some, it would seem that the aim is to "push the boundaries", or to break all the rules. But this would be trying to make a statement *about* art, and not a useful one at that. Similarly, we see attempts to elicit shock out of one's audiences or the public: explicit images, extreme violence, depraved or debased behaviour, or the reduction to simply anything that gets noticed. Such come across most strongly as an attention seeking effort by the artist. We couldn't categorise either as a noble pursuit, so would not befit the more important role that we seek. As for the artistic merit of such tactics, I believe Busoni summarised it most succinctly:

> *"The creator should take over no traditional law in blind belief, which would make him view his own creative endeavour, from the outset, as an exception contrasting with that law. For his individual case he should seek out and formulate a fitting individual law, which, after the first complete realization, he should annul, that he himself may not be drawn into repetitions when his next work shall be in the making.*
>
> *The function of the creative artist consists in making laws, not in following laws ready made. He who follows such laws, ceases to be a creator.*
>
> *Creative power may be the more readily recognized, the more it shakes itself loose from tradition. But an intentional avoidance of the rules cannot masquerade as creative power, and still less engender it.*
>
> *The true creator strives, in reality, after perfection only. And through bringing this into harmony with his own individuality, a new law arises without premeditation."*

This lays down quite a challenge for the artist. But it is a challenge that any true artist will immediately recognise and relish.

And thus we see that the true artist is he who furnishes some kind of order out of the chaos. An impulse to break everything down and return all to chaos is not an artistic one. Nor, in any real sense, is it skilful or challenging. And here we reconvene with our earlier assertion. The sciences give us adequate descriptions of the action of the physical universe: it tends toward entropy. The physical universe seems bound upon a quest to render all into chaos. That which works in the opposite direction, creating order in a myriad of forms, is life.

The revolutionary, bent on destruction rather than creation, will often seek to tear down the new ruling party as soon as the old one has been overthrown. It is the nature of revolution that he aligns with, not the lofty ideals. Although, political activism holds a pivotal function in society, whether it be waving placards, exposing unacceptable conditions through photography, peaceful demonstrations, challenging oppressive regulations through song and speech, or lobbying for law changes. Furthermore it is the right of every citizen to get involved if he wishes, and the artist is certainly not excluded.

But there is another perspective to consider. My Grandfather died when I was still a child, so I unfortunately never got to know him as a man. By all accounts, he was a true war hero, completing a full twenty-two year military service and being decorated with a whole string of medals. During the Second World War he was a paratrooper, dropped in behind enemy lines, only to be hit by machine gun fire as he descended over a field. The bullet went straight through his right arm, into his chest and clean out the other side, yet he survived, was captured, and was taken prisoner of war.

Although, the enduring memories that I have of him concern his reluctance to talk about his ordeals. He never attended any of the Remembrance Day parades and used to curse at them when they appeared on the television. "What do they want to keep bringing it up for?" he would admonish, "Yes, I was in the war. It was horrible. Can't we let it be in the past where it belongs?"

At the primary school I attended, we were covering the topic of the Second World War, and as part of a project we were encouraged to gather experiences of people who were alive at the time. Naturally, I went to see my Grandfather, who, after a fashion, consented to help, no doubt feeling obliged to do so through the family bond. But he was noticeably irritated; his feelings summed up in his rhetorical question: "Why do they want to fill children's heads full of all that rubbish?"

If we are to believe that coverage of these subjects is necessary in order to "learn from the lessons of the past", then as a species we certainly haven't gotten the message so far. And it is not through a lack of talking about them. The sentiment is understandable, but it could be the case that rather than learning from history and moving on, we are anchoring ourselves to it.

An experiment that can be performed is to say to a work colleague, when he first arrives in the morning, "hey, are you feeling OK? You look rather ill". No doubt he'll dismiss these words and assert he is fine. If another person comes up and tells him he looks sick, he is likely to shrug that off too. Once he has had everyone he meets in the office that day enquire after his health and tell him how rough he is looking, he's not so sure, and actually starts to feel a bit under the weather. The next day he doesn't show up for work as he has come down with a cold.

I don't suggest you actually perform this experiment, by the way – it's a cruel trick to play on anyone. But it may imply that if you go around hammering into people that they are downtrodden and oppressed, they'll start to believe that too. In some cases, this may be a much-needed wake up call, but in others it may become a self-fulfilling prophecy.

For the recovering alcoholic who can't go anywhere near a drink, smell it, or even look at pictures of it, his life is still ruled by alcohol. The more impassioned are the ravings of the atheist, the more strenuously he insists on the existence of a God – that he doesn't believe in. He will tell you everything about that God, which he will then deny. And so the reactionary is defined by that which he is kicking against, whether this be politically, socially, or stylistically in his artistic pursuit. To oppose a rule is to be, at least to some degree, still bound by it. Rules are not made to be broken, but to be ignored. The alternative, as is illustrated by Busoni, is to create something better. What you focus on is what you are likely to get.

So we have two approaches to bringing changes for the future. Both are valid and have workability in appropriate places. Raising awareness of unwanted conditions can bring about their transformation, but runs the risk of strengthening the belief in and acceptance of those same conditions. Focusing on the creation of a desirable future can bring it into fruition, but can fall prey to "whistling past the graveyard"[13]. Used wisely they could both be beneficial, used unwisely they could both be detrimental. So where does the responsibility of the artist lie?

A clue is to be found in the fact that art is usually deemed to be a creative activity. Activism is generally a destructive activity – seeking to take down that to which one is opposed. It is engaged upon when necessary, but usually doesn't form one's main occupation. Inciting riots and motivating men into battle could hardly be called a harmonious endeavour. Whenever we attack we are dealing in divisions – barriers of separation.

A powerful artistic experience, however, is capable of producing the "oceanic feeling" – the sense of a "oneness with everything". It tends to dissolve barriers and unite, opening the door to new possibilities. The artist can do much to carry people forward – not just picking them up from the mud, but taking them to the stars.

---

13 Attempting to stay cheerful or hoping for the best while ignoring an imminent danger or grim situation.

There are more subtle issues which rear their head in the "art is not a statement" debate – sometimes unexpectedly. To conclude this chapter, I shall give an account of a time I became aware that I had fallen foul of this slippery character.

Several years ago I was out at a gig, and during the interval I was talking with the guitarist, Andrew, when the subject of poetry entered the conversation. I expressed that I had never really "gotten into it". Not that I had made a real effort to discover poetry, or even read a huge amount of it, but I hadn't gotten a lot out of what I had encountered. Andrew's reply served to be a singular piece of advice: "The thing I find about poetry, is, to *just read it*. Don't try to scrutinize every line and work out the meaning. I find it much more enjoyable when I just read it".

This instantly struck a chord, as that is exactly the mistake I had been making: approaching poems as if they were works of philosophy, and coming away underwhelmed and a trifle bamboozled. The folly of my ways was immediately apparent, as it finally dawned on me that poetry is an aesthetic pursuit; an art form that should be experienced like any other, not dissected.

Shortly after that brief conversation, with this fresh perspective in mind and a newly-obtained copy of T.S. Elliot poetry in hand (Andrew had mentioned him as being a favourite), I read through the first poem, and was blown away. I had been pacing through the house whilst reading, but as I approached the end of the piece I became rooted to the spot and remained there for what must have been several minutes after its conclusion in a state of silent reverie beyond description. The world of poetry had been opened up to me.

I had made the mistake of thinking poetry had to be delivering a statement, rather than appreciating it for what it is.

Eleven Things That Art is Not

Chapter 7

The Seventh *Not*

A solidly constructed kitchen table may be produced with great care, attention, and no small degree of skill. It may have been made by a master table maker, fully apprenticed in the generations-old family tradition, and with the best quality materials. It may inspire in the cook a confidence of stability and usefulness, as she merrily chops the carrots and kneads the dough. But it is unlikely to inspire a change in the direction of one's life. It's a table.

Similarly, the meal that was prepared upon said table could have been a work of culinary expertise. The very aroma drifting through from the kitchen had the whole family's nostrils twitching in delight and stomachs turning cartwheels of anticipation. Every last morsel was hungrily wolfed by the diners as though it were their last, to the accompaniment of smacking lips and rousing plaudits to the chef. Nobody, however, was propelled through a full gamut of emotions. Nobody had an omniscient vision of the universe and their place in it. It was a meal. It tasted delicious and was thoroughly nutritious –

everything you could hope for from a good meal. Food, however much we may dress it up, plays a very straightforward role in human societies.

Millions are allocated in design budgets for televisions, stereos, microwave ovens, toasters. Some may look attractive in the home. But seldom do they afford a revelation of the divine. All such activities have their admirable qualities and their practitioners deserve the appropriate praise for their efforts. However:

Art is *not* craftsmanship.

This topic may cause ructions in some quarters, yet no attempt is being made to defame great works of craftsmanship. On the contrary, if we are to be clearer about our definitions, it may not only be inappropriate to call a skilful work of craftsmanship "art", but also an insult to do so. For we would not only be misconstruing the nature of art, but also failing to recognise the true merits of craftsmanship. It would be unfair to reduce their trade to the sense of some ethereal "gift". Make no mistake, they've worked hard and taken great care to master their craft.

A recent visit to the famous Art Institute of Chicago served to illustrate the extent of this confusion. Alongside the magnificent works on display were exhibitions from various parts of the world featuring primitive hand tools, suits of armour, crude weapons of war, plain earthenware pots that clearly served as nothing but basic cooking implements, and other simple, undecorated, household items of days gone by. These articles were not conceived as works of art, were not regarded as artworks in their time, did not fulfil artistic purposes in their working lives, and have nothing artistic about them in the here and now. What were they doing there? Perhaps more tellingly, why does the inclusion of these irrelevant articles fail to bat more eyelids? Such objects may be at home in a historical museum, but surely not an art institute. One wonders if the curators have lost sight of the role of their establishment.

It needs to be pointed out that there is a definition of art which relates directly to the *artisan*, and reads along the lines of "a skill acquired through practice". This would concern tradesmen of all description. Let us understand this is a different definition for the word than the one we are dealing with in this book.

Another approach to the whole idea of stripping off the *nots* from art could be to assign a new term for the particular kind of artwork we are referring to, and to promote that in conjunction with appropriate boundaries of demarcation. Were we to do this, however, it is likely to follow the same fate as the current term, and where we have had a perfectly good word, with all the positive connotations that it has rightfully acquired over time, there is no need to change it. There is also no guarantee that a new term would catch on, language being such a fickle and recalcitrant entity in the hands of human populations.

So we need to recognise which definition we are using when we speak of the sportsman and his art. The professional athlete is exhibiting a fantastic degree of hard-earned skill. This is the art of a craftsman at work. I love sports – I've played them, watched them and enjoyed them all my life. There are many benefits to participation in sports: health and fitness, developing team work, socialising and camaraderie. They provide a channel for the competitive streak in man which is preferable to fighting and wars. Yet however much we appreciate the skill and craftsmanship involved, I'll wager that the Prime Experience which came to mind for you wasn't a snooker player hitting a high break[14].

---

14 Snooker is a game, similar to pool and billiards, played on a table with balls that are "potted" into holes known as "pockets" by using a "cue" (long pole of wood). A successful consecutive run of "pots" is called a "break", and a "high break" scores a lot of points and demonstrate quite a

We are not limiting this discussion to any particular discipline. As suggested in the chapter on "Art is not entertainment", painting is a form of art, but not all painting is art. The painter or photographer commissioned for a portrait is usually being employed for his craftsmanship. He is not necessarily being employed as an artist, and his final product, however satisfactory it is and regardless of how happy the customer may be, may not enter into the realm of art.

As well as freeing up art from the unwarranted associations, we are also freeing up other domains from the unwarranted association of art. Personally, I like cooking, and I thoroughly appreciate superior cuisine. But it does not have to be "art". Let us look upon it in a frame of reference that is applicable, justified and useful. It should be good quality produce, well cooked and pleasingly presented.

There is, having said all this, an essential element of skill in the creation of a work of art. If you lack the vocabulary and grammatical sense needed to transfuse the atmosphere of the opening scene into your reader's mind, you are forever going to struggle to tell that story. Physical adroitness and dexterity are required for the melody to flow straight from your consciousness, through your instrument, and out into the airwaves, or for your mind's eye to travel along your paintbrush to the canvas. The degree to which your tools present a physical barrier to you is the degree to which the pipeline of your artistic output will be constricted. We don't want any bottlenecks, so the artist needs to be a craftsman *as well* – the goal being to know your tools well enough that they become a part or extension of you. But this does not mean that everything you do with those tools from then on will be great art, or even art at all, regardless of how much skill you have acquired to dazzle your friends.

Although the focus in this slender chapter was on separating out

---

degree of skill. No particular significance is intended, as any act of sporting prowess could be substituted into this sentence.

definitions, it has not been an exercise in semantics. The intention of this book, as a whole, is not to play word games. We are after something. To chase it down, we need to get at the underlying purposes, mechanisms and roles, to which there is a greater distinction than the pinning of name tags. The "art" of the craftsman and the "art" of your Prime Experience may share a homonymic link, but they lie worlds apart below the surface. And so we continue our excavation.

Eleven Things That Art is Not

Chapter 8

The Eighth *Not*

Antoine du Saint Exupery, in his book *Wind, Sand and Stars*, gives an account of when he was engaged as a pilot for the airmail runs going from France, over the Spanish mountains, and into Africa. This occupation was fraught with danger, it being soberingly common for a plane to not return home and never be heard from again. The pilots of this crew were hardened characters who accepted their battles with the elements and near-collisions with death as part of the job. They seldom relayed details of their treacherous encounters to others, and du Saint Exupery gives one explanation why:

> *"The cyclone of which I am about to speak was, physically, much the most brutal and overwhelming experience I ever underwent; and yet beyond a certain point I do not know how to convey its violence except by piling one adjective on another, so that in the end I should convey no impression at all – unless perhaps that of an embarrassing taste for exaggeration.*

> *It took me some time to grasp the fundamental reason for this powerlessness, which is simply that I should be trying to describe a catastrophe that never took place. The reason why writers fail when they attempt to evoke horror is that horror is something invented after the fact, when one is re-creating the experience over again in the memory. Horror does not manifest itself in the world of reality"*

He proceeds to give a remarkably honest account of the ordeal, returning to highlight this counter-intuitive notion of being unfazed by the imminent peril. At the key moment of receiving the first, sudden blast from the cyclone, when all around him "blew up", he recounts:

> *"Concerning the next couple of minutes I have nothing to say. All that I can find in my memory is a few rudimentary notions, fragments of thoughts, direct observations. I cannot compose them into a dramatic recital because there was no drama. The best I can do is line them up in a kind of chronological order."*

The sequence of events that he continues to recount would give ample material for an action scene in a Hollywood thriller, or rousing climax to an adventure novel, yet du Saint Exupery continues:

> *"Still nothing pathetic to report. I was wrestling with chaos, was wearing myself out in a battle with chaos, struggling to keep in the air a gigantic house of cards that kept collapsing despite all I could do. Scarcely the faintest twinge of fear went through me when one of the walls of my prison rose suddenly like a tidal wave over my head. My heart hardly skipped a beat when I was tripped up by one of the whirling eddies of air that the sharp ridge darted into my ship. If I felt anything unmistakable in the haze of confused feelings and notions that came over me each time*

one of these powder magazines blew up, it was a feeling of respect. I respected that sharp-toothed ridge. I respected that peak. I respected that dome. I respected that transversal valley opening out into my valley and about to toss me God knew how violently as soon as its torrent of wind flowed into the one on which I was being borne along."

More calamity, now being flung back out to sea with little hope of safely reaching the shore, facing the prospect of an untimely end at the bottom of the ocean, and still:

"I hung on, meanwhile, to the controls of my heavy transport plane, my attention monopolized by the physical struggle and my mind occupied by the very simplest thoughts. I was feeling practically nothing as I stared down at the imprint made by the wind on the sea."

The sheer intensity of the experience appeared to keep the terror of the situation at bay. This becomes evident through the next passage:

"There were moments of respite, nevertheless. I dare say those moments themselves were the equal to the worst storms I had hitherto met, but by comparison with the cyclone they were moments of relaxation...

...Then, in those moments, I began to feel I was doomed. Then was the time that little by little I began to tremble for myself. So much so that each time I saw the unfurling of a new white offensive I was seized by a brief spasm of panic which lasted until the exact instant when, on the edge of that bubbling cauldron, I bumped into the invisible wall of wind. That restored me to numbness again."

113

After miraculously making it to the shore, he walked off from the platoon of soldiers that had been sent to watch out for him, feeling he had nothing to say:

> *"I could not collect my thoughts enough to decide whether or not I had been afraid. Had I been afraid? I couldn't say.*
>
> *"The day after I landed I might get emotional, might dress up my adventure by imagining that I who was alive and walking on earth was living through the hell of a cyclone. But that would be cheating, for the man who had fought tooth and nail against that cyclone had nothing in common with the fortunate man alive the next day. He was far too busy."*

Sudden bad news may bring one to tears. But the tears flow once the message has "sunk in". At the receipt point, there is nothing, or what some may describe as being "stunned". The joy of winning a race comes with the relief after having crossed the finishing line. During the race, the runner is much too focused on the task at hand; they are "in the zone".

Through the arts we may experience similar joys and sadnesses. We may cry in response to a work itself, or it may help us to release the pent-up emotions of a distressing situation. Art may provide us with delight, or resonate with our own; accordingly, heightening it to exhilaration.

> *"Art is a human activity having for its purpose the transmission to others of the highest and the best feelings to which men have risen."*

Chapter 8: The Eighth Not

"By words one transmits thoughts to another; by means of art, one transmits feelings."

(Leo Tolstoy)

Tolstoy is here moving on from the assertion that art is a communication, and is specialising it as a communication of emotion. He is not alone in this assertion. Many have proposed similar conclusions, or stated that art is all about emotion or even that art *is* the emotional response that it arouses. But, as you may have already guessed, we are about to realign these assertions:

Art is *not* emotion.

Obviously, we are not divorcing emotion from art altogether, as they doubtless share a close relationship. But a relationship it is, not an identity. The examples above show us how emotion accompanies many of man's activities, although at least for intense experiences, it usually does so after the fact of the significant event, one might almost say as a by-product. We could debate whether the same delayed reaction occurs in day-to-day activities. Emotion may appear to run concurrent to some circumstances, or prior to them in the case of anxieties and anticipations, however in general it arises as a response to a situation. In either case we are not interested, because we are dealing with art which, as has been covered earlier, is no minor incident.

Is it possible to have art without emotion? Perhaps. Perhaps not. It is not a question that is likely to lead anywhere revealing. We shall take another approach.

Consider the diagram on the following page:

115

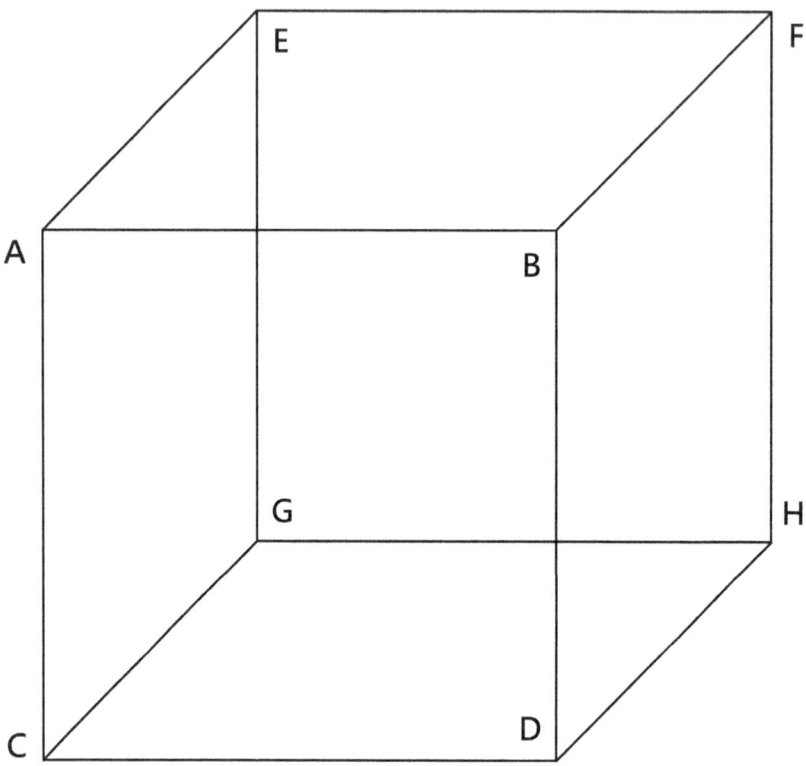

This is a familiar representation of a cube. It can, however, be interpreted in more than one way. A cube may be seen with the square ABCD at the front, appearing as though looking down on the cube. It can also be seen as though looking up at the cube, with the square EFGH as the front side. Convince yourself this is so, then do the following exercise, using the image below which has omitted the labels so they don't get in the way.

Chapter 8: The Eighth Not

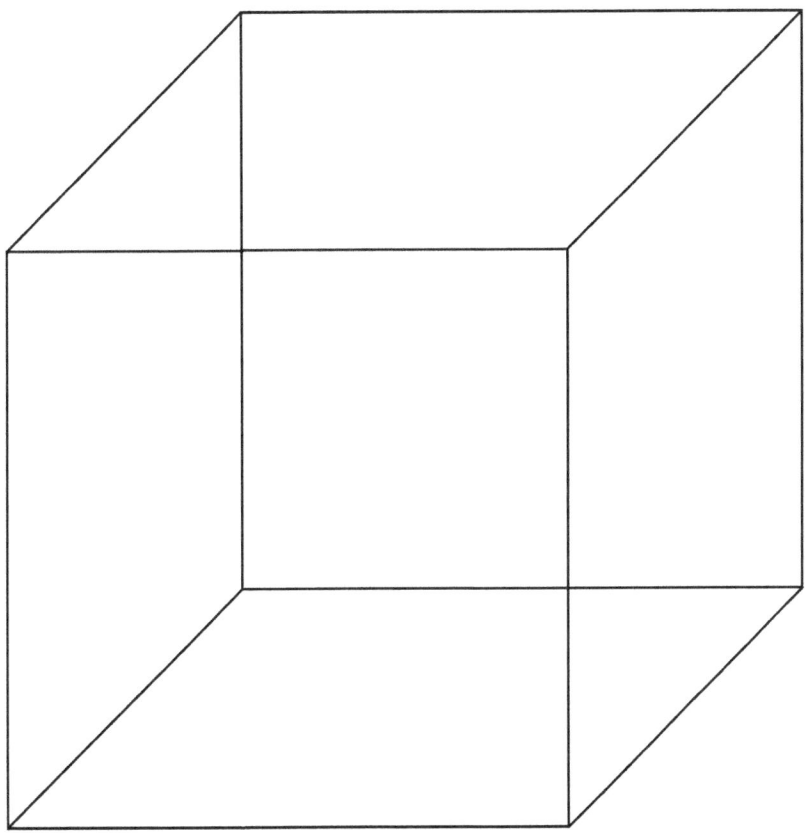

Focus on one of the interpretations of a cube – whichever one comes most naturally to you. Now *slowly,* change it to the other one.

How was that? Anything happen there? If you managed to do this, and at a slow pace, you may have experienced a point where there was neither one cube nor the other. Interesting phenomena can surround this point, where one is floating between concepts, paused on the stream of consciousness in a kind of dead time where everything else appears to stand still. This moment may have passed very quickly for some, almost unnoticed, yet for others it may have seemed to linger for an indeterminate period, and can even make one quite disoriented.

It is this point, this state of consciousness (or no-consciousness, depending on how you look at it), which is cultivated by mystics and is the goal of meditation – a state where one is free of thought. There are many techniques associated with meditation: repeating mantras, breathing exercises, counting, focusing on a point inside one's head, etc. It would be a mistake, however, to confuse these with the actual state of meditation. The techniques are merely aids to quieting the mind, and as this is achieved the techniques should fall away.

The idea is not totally alien to Western philosophy. Hegel wrote that "pure being and pure nothing are one and the same". Heidegger concurred with this proposition, adding that "Nothing, not merely provides the conceptual opposite of what is, but is also an original part of essence". Rejecting the notion of subject/object duality in favour of states and actions, he saw a path to reaching the "pure being" through "...the thorough examination and absorption into emotions such as boredom or dread".

The means by which it is entered are largely irrelevant – the goal is the state between concepts, which is all the more readily demonstrated by our cube example as we are using non-verbal concepts.

Note that, along with an absence of mind, there also manifests an absence of emotion. It would be a mistake, however, to assume that nothing happens at this point. This would be like assuming that there is no energy or power in a vacuum – a mistake indeed. As an illustration, imagine you were looking down a street with high-rise buildings. There is a static rope stretching across the road in front of you, disappearing out of view on either side. With nothing observably moving on the street, you may be inclined to think there is nothing happening, however what you don't see is the two teams of men down the side streets, heaving at the rope in an evenly matched "tug of war" battle. There is a profusion of potential energy.

The purpose of this exercise has not been to convince everyone they should be meditating. What we are interested in is that it can tell us something about art. In your Prime Experience, was there not a moment like this, that was beyond emotion? A "time stops still" moment, devoid of thought?

Let's examine thought itself a little more closely. As part of a natural process, we forge mental links between items in order to build up knowledge and understanding. Mapping of facts to other facts helps us to draw conclusions, assimilate our sensory input and predict consequences. We can see this in action if we observe a social conversation, where related slices of personal experience are fired off in the minds of the participants, causing the discussion to meander from topic to topic. Bob tells about a recent trip to Peru, which triggers a memory in Sally, who says she studied about Peru when she was in University. Jane says she studied Chemistry at University, and the conversation moves onto Chemistry.

Sometimes the link is a tenuous one and, not recognising it, we see the comment as being out of place. Fred, recalling the chemistry set he was given for his 7th birthday which his big brother smashed to pieces, interjects "you know, I really hated my brother", and receives a puzzled frown from Bob, Sally and Jane.

So the process is generally useful, nay essential, however it can be detrimental when erroneous associations are made or when associations are used in circumstances for which they are not appropriate.

Most of us have an internal dialogue or "stream of consciousness" in which the passage of our thoughts appear to us in words. Here we can observe our personal pattern of associations as we mentally wander from subject to subject. Learning new information and generating new ideas usually involves creating new associations between previously unrelated pieces of data. "Thinking out of the box" generally means breaking free from habitual modes of thought, from following the same pathway of associations, to seek out new connections. There will be more on this later, but the point being focused on here is that to get "out of the box" requires a suspension of this internal stream of associations. One must see beyond the confines of the modes of thought which have become ingrained in the individual, culture or race.

It has often been noted how great discoveries commonly come about when the scientist or inventor is engaged in entirely different activities, and are therefore suspending their conscious attention from their work. The moments of enlightenment come, not when pouring over the work bench, but when out strolling through the woods or sailing down the river, when one's mind is entirely off the task. A psychologist would see these new ideas as coming from the "unconscious mind" – a storehouse of information free of the usual associations, enabling new connections to be made.

We have a parallel in our cube example where we are able, for a moment at least, to view the diagram in its purity, without the filter of one concept or another. Is the glass half full or half empty? The ultimate answer is: neither; it just *is*. The associations are put on afterwards and cause us to see things a certain way. Dreams are often seen as a playground for creativity, as the rules of the game are not so fixed and allow us to explore associations that would either not occur to us at other times or would appear absurd.

Given the simultaneity of discoveries, as alluded to earlier, we could conceive these new connections as coming from a "universal mind" or "collective consciousness", which we are somehow able to tap. We could see them as being touched by God – whatever you perceive Him to be. Perhaps through the stillness we transcend the physical universe – opening up a portal to experience another realm. However we choose to look at it, we are dipping into a well, accessible via a transcendence of emotion and thought.

It is this contact with the great unknown, the void of potentiality, from which new order arises, new perspectives, new understandings. And it is this significant event which needs to be the focus of our examination of art. Art orients us toward the state of "pure being"; that is, art orients us towards life. Emotional reactions may follow in the wake of these moments of crystallization, to the point of being overwhelming. They contribute to the power of the experience, perhaps providing relief for what may otherwise be unnerving disruptions of our stably-held beliefs, and they let us know that something significant has happened. The significant events themselves, we shall return to in a later chapter.

Eleven Things That Art is Not

Chapter 9

The Ninth *Not*

To recap on the introduction, artists have been held in varying regards over the ages, and their roles in society have clearly changed. We don't know the full extent of their status or influence in the ancient world, although from what we can observe in the remnants of these societies it was considerable. From the middle ages up to the latter parts of the last millennium in Europe, aside from some indigenous folk musics and the such like, professional artists were usually employed by the church or noble patrons, and the influence is generally reflected in the orientation of most of the art work which remains from these periods.

Come the end of the eighteen hundreds, Ludwig van Beethoven was to change the state of play. Hired to play piano for a court of the nobility, he was in the middle of one of his compositions when a young count started to talk over the music. Any other musician, acutely aware of their lowly, expendable position, would have carried on, taken their pay at the end of the gig, and gone about their way with their job intact. Not Beethoven. He stood up, slammed down the lid of the piano and, before storming out of the concert hall, indignantly proclaimed that he refused to perform for such a swine.

Anyone would think that he would never work again in that town, which happened to be Vienna in Austria – more or less the capital of the music world at that time. But that wasn't what happened. Beethoven, who was already making a name for himself, saw his popularity soar like never before. His unshakable belief in the importance of what he was doing made him incapable of adopting a subservient role to anyone. Couched in his own words:

> "There are and always will be thousands of princes, but there is only one Beethoven!"

So great was his integrity, not to mention his compositions and performances, that people started to listen to him, and attitudes towards the artists' place in society began to change. Beethoven himself demanded equality and respect from noble patrons and went on to become the first composer in history to make a successful living from independent publications and commissions, rather than through an exclusive patron.

Whereas this signified a great step forward for the individual artist, it has not come without a cost – "cost", here, being an operative word. As price tags increase, so too do the glittering prizes, the distractions, and the interests of anyone seeking to make a penny. There is no doubt that money, along with its benefits, has its drawbacks. It brings distortions and confusions to any field it infiltrates, clouding over the scene and obscuring what may lie below.

Art is *not* a business.

We have touched upon this subject already, but are now going to give it more thorough coverage by dealing with a different couple of aspects and ramifications.

It is only for the last hundred years or so, aided by some technological developments, that the arts have moved into a largely commercial framework. The ability to record images, sound and film, along with advances in global communications, commerce and distribution, has converted what were once localised, live performances and artistic creations into products which could be exported, widely advertised and traded on open markets. Many companies were spawned and built up over the ensuing decades to take advantage of these new enterprises, and the massive art and media industries that we see today came into existence.

Signs have been gathering for some time that this period has run its course and is coming to an end. The digital revolution, along with the plus points mentioned earlier, has also brought with it challenges to the operating basis of the last century. The business models that the industry leaders have profited from greatly no longer appear viable. We are living in a world where products which once required heavy funding to produce, market and distribute, are now able to be created and made available to a world-wide audience at the click of a button, and at virtually no cost.

Now that the initial shock wave has reverberated round the globe from such a relatively sudden upheaval, new models are beginning to appear. The multinational companies, however, are still attempting to clamp down on what they perceive to be threats to their existence – calling for new laws governing digital media and ever more comprehensive copyright restrictions. The industry that convinced everybody to exchange their beloved record collections for cheaper to produce (but more expensive to buy) CDs, is currently performing a desperate back-peddle to try and push everyone back onto vinyl again. It is debatable whether the sound quality is superior – the move smacks more of a yearning for the "good old days" when they had records flying off the shelves. It's not so easy to make copies of vinyl.

Instead of swimming against the tide, some musicians have embraced the new technologies and evaluated the advantages that it gives them. In years gone by, a band had to be signed to a label if they hoped to release any records. Recording studios were expensive – way out of the budget of your average group. Getting the records manufactured was similarly expensive and would require a large investment. The final product had to be distributed, which also meant developing relationships with retailers, and of course, it had to be advertised in the right places – more money and contacts.

In many respects, this has radically changed. Bands can get good quality recordings at affordable prices, even with home studio setups. The internet provides the means for uploading and distributing music to a global market without any manufacturing or distribution costs, and there are many avenues for advertisement. A result of this is that much of the money has dropped out of the recorded music scene. Apart from a small percentage, however, most musicians never saw much of the record sales anyway. Where they were successful they made money from royalty payments, selling merchandise and live performances. The move made by some forward-thinking musicians is to make their music freely available for anybody to download on the internet, and putting down any negligible costs incurred in the creation of the recordings as advertising. The idea behind this is to build up and encourage a fan base in order to boost attendances at their live concerts.

To contrast these progressive thinkers with the old guard, this chapter was originally introduced by an appropriate quote from an old song. After finally tracking down the organisation handling the publishing rights for the lyrics, a request for permission to use it was answered with minimum charge of several hundred dollars. The single sentence would add no monetary value to the product whatsoever, so it was simply removed. One would have thought that the band would appreciate a little tribute and a bit of free advertising for a song that is now over thirty years old and is either unknown or forgotten about by practically everybody. Presenting a fee that is obviously prohibitive misses out on the opportunity and is suggestive of a decision made by persons attempting to make a quick buck off the back of the artists, rather than the artists themselves.

An increasing number of writers are independently publishing their works. Again, they can take advantage of the global reach of the internet to provide online downloads of eBooks without the costs of printing and distributing paper books. There are also avenues for getting physical books printed affordably, as well as access to editing facilities and all the other services that would have traditionally been provided by a publisher.

There are other business models emerging. Some artists are following an online trend of making digital products free to download and asking for donations. There are streaming sites which pay royalties for repeated views of uploaded content. Sites such as Patreon and Kickstarter are providing platforms for artists to receive funding directly from people who are interested in their work and wish to support them. It must be said, however, that these efforts currently still only account for a tiny percentage of the market share, as will be covered below. We are very much in a transitional phase, and many more models are likely to appear and disappear before the dust settles.

There is no suggestion being made that the middlemen are all evil – like some insidious strain that need to be purged and sent to oblivion to stop them infecting the pure, idealised world of saintly artists. They have served their purpose too. In the main, artists are notoriously poor at business, and without people behind them we wouldn't have been made aware of the household names that have inspired us over generations. If you wish to purchase a painting, you will preferably want to see it in person. It's just not the same looking at a digital representation on a computer screen. Galleries are therefore very useful, and in the current society in which we live, gallery owners also need to earn a living.

A drawback to the industries of art, however, is the inevitable effect on the content of what becomes the "mainstream". Companies are formed to make money. They have to be profitable to survive. This means that companies, especially as they increase in size, are naturally going to focus on producing products for the widest customer base possible. The food and clothing industries thrive because we all wear clothes and we all need to eat every day. But the *Pogo Stick* industry is not set for world domination.

Recognising this fact, art industry companies will centre upon art works that they believe will have broad public appeal. A national company wants products it can sell to the nation, and an international one wants to sell to the world. Attempting to please everyone all of the time, however, unavoidably results in the lowest common denominator.

When a new style or genre develops within any of the arts it usually does so in a localised area, supported by a minority of enthusiasts, initially composed of the artists themselves, and later by a small core of, usually ardent, fans. This is the stage where exciting things happen. Fresh ideas freely flow as artists experiment with and come to define the boundaries and intents of the emerging form of expression. It may be raw, it may be edgy, but it's real and it's *alive*. The culture which grows up around the new scene is buzzing, vibrant and bursting with energy.

But it will take quite some time and will have to spread a considerable degree before any of the mainstream are willing to take a risk on it. They're not interested in selling to the few hundred diehards, they want to sell to the millions, so are not about to weigh in with any serious investment. Eventually, if the scene develops enough of a following, it will start to filter into the mainstream, but this will usually take the form of some watered-down elements of the genre adapted to fit a "commercially acceptable" style – art with all the crusts cut off to make sure it won't hurt anybody. Often the essence of what originally made the genre good is totally absent.

By the time the world comes to know of it, the artists who instigated the genre have usually moved on somewhere else. And so will have many of the original supporters, frustrated by all the groupies of this "new" mainstream genre which doesn't bear much resemblance to the "real" scene that they fell in love with. In this way there is always an underground – shifting, bubbling, morphing. The mainstream is where art forms solidify into static forms – proven formulas for proven saleability and proven profits.

Of course, some genres forever stay on the fringes, as they are deemed "too hot to handle" or not "trendy" enough by the mainstream, and the general public remains unaware of their existence. And, naturally, there are exceptions. Some great artists do make it into the mainstream, albeit with varying degrees of compromise.

Another factor compounds the issue. Although the food, clothes and other industries thrive, with a wide selection of manufacturers, retailers and distributors all vying for our business, there are actually only a handful of companies present in your average high street. And it is the same companies that are present in the next town, and the one after that. The smaller companies are owned by larger companies, who in turn are subsidiaries of even larger companies.

And so it is with the art industries. There are only six record companies worth speaking of, who between them account for over

129

90% of the business share in music sales. You may hear many other names, but they are all actually subsidiaries of the same big six. There are five large publishing companies and the same situation exists with film companies.

But it goes further than this. The channels through which the world gets to hear about its art, entertainment and culture – the TV stations, newspapers, radio stations, magazines, etc. – are also all controlled by a small handful of media giants. We have more of these outlets than ever, with new ones springing up all the time, providing an illusion of choice. But all the paths and all the road signs are leading to the same few locations.

As an example of the extent of control exerted by these companies, I know someone who was playing in a band back in the 1970's. They were developing quite a following and aroused the interests of record companies, one of which told them that if they signed their contract, they would be at number four in the charts a year from now. One year to the day, they were not at number five in the charts, not at number three, but at number four. And the scene has only gotten worse over the intervening years, not better. Have you ever wondered how "artists" that nobody has previously heard of, never done a gig in their life, can suddenly appear with a single in the top ten?

The conflict of interests makes the situation even more extreme, when you consider that the parent companies of many media corporations are the same as those of the film, publishing and music companies. Whom do you think they are going to promote? Even if there is not a direct link, there are often indirect ones. Commercial TV stations, newspapers and radio stations are funded by advertising. The large multinational corporations tend to have fingers in many pies, with subsidiary companies in a range of industries that advertise through those media outlets. Magazine A is not going to print a negative review for film company B's latest blandbuster, when the advertising keeping them afloat is paid for by film company B's sister company.

Even without the immediate financial links, the art and media industries share a reciprocal relationship. The newspapers, TV and radio stations, magazines, etc. are in a similar position to the film, publishing and music companies. They have to survive, and therefore want to appeal to the masses, not the minorities. They are going to feature whatever the major companies hand them as being the current biggest thing. All the column inches and all the seconds of airtime will be dedicated, almost exclusively, to the output of a small number of international giants.

Given that this mass-media coverage is all that the majority of people are exposed to, these become the products they will buy, watch, read, listen to, etc., and the whole system becomes a self-perpetuating cycle. The public are consistently told what is "cool" and what they should like via sensory overload from every direction until it becomes hypnotic. They buy the products, which supports the companies to fuel another round, along with all the royalties they receive from the airplay.

You may think that things are different now, in this modern world of the internet. Surely, cyberspace is the people's media, championing the decentralisation of power. Well, potentially that could be the case, but in reality, at least at the moment, it isn't. For sure, there is a huge diversification of material available to anyone across the globe, but the truth is that the vast majority of us spend the vast majority of our surfing time on the same few sites. The statistics are even more overwhelming than those of the traditional sales markets. And guess who either owns and controls those sites or pays for all the advertising that funds them. Plus the search algorithms and

131

relevance indicators[15] ensure these sites keep their viewers cocooned in their little bubble – conscious only of the same couple of high streets, and leaving all the back roads, suburbs, country lanes, mountains and oceans unexplored.

One could argue that this is just good business, and from a purely monetary perspective one would have to agree. They have kept this up for a long time and they are very good at it. But there are more drawbacks than those alluded to above. With the majority of people being raised on a diet of shrink-wrapped mediocrity, it becomes difficult to assimilate different or alternative art forms. Anything out of the mainstream will appear so far out of their reality (remember the originality scale spoken of earlier) that they won't be able to relate to it. They have not been exposed to anything that bridges the gap.

The centralisation of attention achieved by the consuming grip of the large companies actually means less choice for many, not more. Most people simply don't know that the products they are aware of through the mainstream account for such a tiny percentage of the enormity of artistic output available. The result is also a stripping away of resources from other areas. When all the money in the collective pot is pocketed by a few individuals, it leaves little for everyone else. Theatre companies struggle to survive, having to put on well-known favourite shows to sell tickets, and being forced into using backing tapes because they can't afford to pay musicians. How many cinemas do you know of that show independently made films? There are fewer professional orchestras around, and those who survive often rely on grants and sponsorship. We see an infestation of "Tribute" acts in venues large and small – reduced to having to impersonate the mainstream stars to try and get a gig and put some bums on seats.

---

15 Some websites will gather information which they use to present content, such as the results of a search, which follow a particular formula and/or are tailored to the individual.

Chapter 9: The Ninth Not

The world of contemporary art and the industry which has built up around it has performed a further abstraction. Here we do see what could be considered the "cutting edge" making it to the fore, however this is frequently in the guise of sensationalism. But the singular phenomenon to note is that the consumers of these works, the major art collectors, often have no regard whatsoever for the pieces they are buying. They pay the massively over-inflated price tags either as a pure investment or, as they tend to openly admit, because of the status that will be afforded them by doing so. What we end up with is the whole complex sphere of auction houses, publicity gurus, critics, galleries and collectors, orbiting around the binary star of money and notoriety, all with the impression of being centred around art but in actuality having very little, if anything, to do with it.

One cannot really blame the artists for the fads and fashions that dominate this strangely abstracted marketplace, although some do deliberately court it. The disproportionate rewards are obvious for those very few who are lucky enough to be caught up in the whirlwind of hot air.

An area that is flourishing around the arts, and one where a lot of artists end up in order to pay the bills, is education. Art colleges, drama schools and music schools abound, churning out an endless parade of hopefuls with nowhere to go at the end of it. I recall an old-timer talking of the live music scene in the UK, saying "there used to be 100,000 musicians and 50,000 jobs. Now there's a million musicians and 10,000 jobs". There are many reasons behind this decline, however, which is too specialised for us to explore any further here.

What we can explore is the effects of an industry that is interested in marketable products rather than fostering talent. Fame becomes senior to ability, hence a "personality" receives opportunities for which they are utterly undeserving, and the public learns to accept poor

133

quality substitutes for the real thing. TV actors turn their unskilful hands to making pop records. Chefs, "celebrities" and politicians are encouraged to chance their arm at dancing in front of the nation, watched by millions who have never heard of and wouldn't even think of going to see the professionals at work. Publishing houses will hand you a book deal if you are famous, whether or not you are able to write. Hollywood makes star careers for models, sportsman, and even bodybuilders in roles for which they are clearly unsuited. Despite the coaching, generous editing, special effects and the number of takes required to get it right, the ineptitude shines through. Cringe-worthy indeed, when there are scores of fine actors, who gain little or no recognition, giving stellar performances every night of the week in front of live audiences in theatres across the land.

The world of fine art is not immune to the cult of celebrity. Fashionable personalities procure undue attention from the mainstream media which raises them to a lofty status, and their pieces to even loftier price tags. All about the "who" rather than the "what". Karaoke is now routinely advertised as "live music" – an absurdity which goes unnoticed by a populace used to seeing their idols miming to backing tracks on the television, or the wannabes competing to be voted in as the next big stars.

Naturally, the big companies, expert in marketing, advertising, persuasion and the like, use all the tricks to promote their chosen ones. The more videos you can make with provocative dancers wearing next to nothing, the better – whatever product you are trying to market. Artistic content can take second place, or third, or fourth.

I was booked for a gig not long ago to play with a band at the end of a celebration dinner for a dance academy. While we were waiting to go on, there was a performance given by some of the students at the school – a troop of young girls, I estimate around 11-15 years of age, wearing very skimpy and revealing costumes. They proceeded to work through an extended routine of provocative dance in the style of a modern pop video, with all the gyrations, thrusts and innuendo that you might expect to accompany one of the baser examples of its kind. I felt positively uncomfortable, and the feeling was shared by a number of the other band members I was with. This took place in an upmarket hotel, with all the parents sat around taking it all in. It's another aspect of our modern society which we seem to have become deadened to and accept as normal, but I, for one, don't like to see it go that way.

We can't blame the girls for wanting to emulate their heroes. After all, this is how the pop culture tells them they should act. One might hope, given that this kind of material is deliberately pitched and aimed at the younger generation, that the purveyors might take a little more responsibility for their actions, but perhaps it's a little too much to expect large corporations to be scrupulous with their morals.

To summarise, the money factor gives rise to competition, which as we have already covered, has no place in art. It sets up the false goals of fame and fortune at the top of the mountain, leading budding creators astray to wander over many a lonely hilltop. You see, artists, as individuals, whether coerced into artistic compromises by big business or not, also get into the trap of wanting to appeal to the masses, and start to try and tailor their output to some imagined idea of what "the people" want. This inevitably results in a regurgitation of what is already "popular", and is therefore usually bland, and lacking in any real substance.

The truly great artist naturally appeals to the masses by getting in touch with themselves and producing what *they* really want. "Is it commercially viable?" is a question that an artist should never ask of themself, nor be called upon to answer. It is the number one stifling choker of creative and aesthetic flow.

The Artist's true role in society vastly exceeds any consideration

135

of mere wealth – either personal or corporate. To see why, it's time to get serious with our final couple of *nots*.

Author's note: That is where I decided to leave this chapter. There is, however, another aspect which really deserves a mention, but which would require a book on its own in order to do it justice. There is a much more sinister side to the world of mass-media entertainments, both big business and state funded, where they have been used by unscrupulous individuals for their own unsavoury ends, largely in the direction of controlling the populace. One could, if interested, begin by looking up the Radio Research Project and the MK-Ultra mind control experiments, and that should lead down a trail (or a rather deep rabbit hole).

Chapter 10

The Tenth *Not*

What does it mean to be creative? This question is taken up by Arthur Koestler in his influential book *The Act of Creation*, where he isolates a common denominator which runs through a full range of creative activities – from humour, to science and invention, to the arts. The definitive factor is the collision of two or more planes of thought, or "matrices" as he refers to them. You are merrily striding down one mental track, when another comes along from the side and smashes into you, fusing the two together with a connection hitherto unnoticed. Koestler describes this as the law of *bisociation* - the new, previously uncomprehended, association of two matrices.

It's easy to see how this accounts for humour. In a joke, there is always a set-up that gets us going down one track: "What's a foot long and slippery?" Followed by a punchline that cuts in from another angle: "A slipper". Apologies for the quality of the joke, but it serves to demonstrate that, prior to the groan, we were probably thinking with different definitions of "foot" and "slippery" before the two planes or matrices came together. Perhaps an image of a snake was conjured, before the mental bubble was burst.

Progressing to the field of scientific discovery, we have the eureka moment of Archimedes, watching the water level rising as he entered his bathtub, and thereby seeing the solution to the task set him by the Tyrant of Syracuse of measuring the volume of his crown. Inventions can generally be traced back to a point of collision between unrelated fields – seeing a new use for something in a different context. Take the understanding that water continually flows downstream, combine it with the concept of a wheel, and one arrives at the invention of a waterwheel.

The fusion of one style of painting with another can produce a third, completely new style of painting. The bisociation of genre with genre have provided the myriad forms of contemporary dance, poetry, performance art, animation, digital art and the like that we see today.

It is a theory with a high degree of workability. Koestler, in his fascinating book, goes well beyond the extreme abbreviation being presented here. Let us be clinical in our understanding, however, that he is talking about the *creative act* as it appears in all its guises, for which the book is an excellent exposition. Clearly, this has an important part to play in art, although:

Art is *not* creativity.

The part that bisociation has to play in art is in artistic *originality*. The theory has great relevance in this domain, but it falls short of explaining what is going on with art and artistic experience in general. Chapter 2 touched upon the subject of originality, pointing out that this isn't a necessary requirement in the reproduction of artistic works. The same piece can be appreciated over and over again and still be a mind-blowing artistic experience. Originality plays an important function, but there's more going on here.

The bisociation theory has a parallel with the Aristotelian syllogism – the drawing of a conclusion from two premises which are assumed to be true – and is subject to some of the same drawbacks. Most obviously, if a creative idea cannot be conceived without the union of two matrices, then where did the original matrix come from? If they be all syntheses of each other, where did it all start? By not allowing for any concept of plain, unadulterated, straight-out-of-nowhere originality, we are not affording the artist the capacity to produce something simply because he wants to or apropos of nothing.

Koestler also imagines two spectra stretching across the creative landscape: one decreasing in "objective verifiability" and increasing in "aesthetic dimension" as we range from chemistry through to fiction; and the other decreasing in "utility" and increasing in "beauty" as we progress from engineering, through crafts, to art. Interesting concept, but the inherent error is that art should not be divorced from truth, nor from utility. As was mentioned in the introduction, it is only in very recent times that there have been attempts to do so and we shall see why this is an error as we progress.

No doubt many new ideas come from recombinations of known data, however introducing new ideas may not always produce a gain:

> *"Music was chaste and modest so long as it was played on simpler instruments, but since it has come to be played in a variety of manners and confusedly, it has lost the mode of gravity and virtue and fallen almost to baseness."*
>
> *(Anicius Manlius Severinus Boethius c. 480-524)*

Koestler does warn about the phenomena, pointing out that for every successful bisociation of scientific importance, there have been countless others which have not led anywhere, and yet others which have been accepted but later proven to be barking up the wrong tree – therefore being damaging to the progress of discovery. The best sounding ideas in the world may not work out in practice.

Thus we see that idea of bisociation in art works well when analysing after the fact in general terms, but it is not practical for addressing a work in progress. It's not likely to do you much good trying to come up with themes, styles or objects to bisociate with each other. You could be at it all day without landing upon any fruitful combinations.

Difficulty also arises when reducing from the general to the specific. You've drawn the first line of a new sketch. Do you need to bisociate with another matrix to draw the second? Or, put another way, say you are doing the same sketch that you have previously done, but decide to change a few of the lines, or add some. Was the collision of planes of thought necessary, or did you just decide it would look better that way?

These examples suggest we are not allowing for the development of a theme. A composer may take a simple melody and, through the course of a piece, write different variations of it, add embellishments, transpose it to other keys, or alter its rhythmic structure. We could suppose that each one of these repetitions required a collision with another plane of thought, and perhaps break it down in a rigid analysis to unveil every microscopic influence, but I can't imagine any composer employing such a stiflingly complex mindset when writing it, nor any musician when playing it. They are more likely to think of it in terms of extending a single plane of thought.

But without wishing to get lost in the details of practical

application, let us return to theory. Koestler points out that the comedian asks us to re-create the bisociative act in our minds in order to "get" the joke. We have to follow his lines of thought and see the point where they collide. The scientist and inventor alike are both inviting us to appreciate the new bisociations they have created in their theories, laws and inventions. To understand the papers they have written or the ingenuity of their designs we have to re-create their mental progression to the convergence of matrices.

As was mentioned in Chapter 4, the artist is not concerned, if he understands his true purpose, in getting someone to re-create his exact thought. He therefore is doing something other than leading people down the collision course to a particular crossroads.

We could postulate the idea of a bisociation between the artist's plane of thought and the art appreciator's plane of thought, but we would be stretching the analogy. What would we even mean by the "artist's matrix"? Can a work of art be reduced to a plane of thought? Besides, art works often have a great impact because they resonate with us; we feel a deep connection with them, not a collision. Seems like we are trying to bend the theory to squeeze it into our scenario, rather than adopting one that encompasses it. We need a new model.

This is where we pick up our discussion from Chapter 8, where we saw that the point of focus for artistic experience was beyond emotion and thought. One could say it is the opposite of a collision – we want the space *between* concepts, not one plane of thought or the other. The artist is inducing a state which transcends these associations, affords a purer glimpse of reality, and thus opens up new possibilities. To explore this any further, we need to take a diversion to examine the subject of *viewpoint*.

When I talk of viewpoint, I am not here referring to any conceptual or figurative definition. We are not discussing opinions or personal preferences; we are talking about purely physical locations in space – a point from which to view.

It is staggering to consider how minutely selective is our view of reality. We may believe we see a wide periphery of our surroundings, but we are actually only focused on a small point at a time, and our eyes are in almost constant motion, shifting from one spot to another to piece together for us a picture of the world. When in the film *Dead Poets Society*, the teacher played by Robin Williams got his students to stand on their desks so they would see the world from a different perspective, he was making a serious point, however comical it may have come across. Depending upon the location from which we are looking, the world really does appear differently. Look out of the window as you take off in an aeroplane and watch the land rapidly drop away. How does it look from up there? Our thinking is going to be affected whether we are looking at the world from the top of a mountain or through the lens of a microscope. At any given point in time, any second that passes, imagine how many different sights there are to view in the town or city where you live; that is, how many snapshots of reality. What would it do to your mindset if you could absorb them all?

The cherry picking of reality is not limited to vision. Out of necessity, our hearing is extremely particular about the sounds that are relayed to our consciousness, or else we would continually be overwhelmed by the cacophony. The environments we habitually frequent are filled with a multitude of audio waves of which we can only be aware of a small fraction. The same is true of smells; virtually every substance around us gives off some kind of aroma. Kinaesthetic sense or "touch" is greatly influenced by the region of the body being used for the touching – some are many times more sensitive than others.

Let's stretch the concept one stage further. In order to see anything at all, our eyes are dependent upon light reflecting off surfaces and into our retinas. What we know of as light is only a tiny portion of the spectrum of electro-magnetic radiation, which includes radio waves, microwaves, X-rays, and the nuclear band of Alpha, Beta and Gamma radiation. These are what we can detect with instruments, but we don't know just how far this spectrum reaches in either direction.

For all that we perceive through our visionary sense we rely upon this slim band of electro-magnetic radiation. Some animals use frequencies out of our range, and therefore "see" a different reality to us, but as far as we know the animal kingdom still utilises only a thin slice of the available spectrum. Bats paint a picture of 3D space with sound. Dogs and elephants have hearing which extends well beyond the human ear, in the higher and lower frequencies respectively. If you have ever observed a cat for any length of time you will have noted that on occasion they appear to see things that none of the rest of us can see. Sharks smell a drop of blood from miles away.

If you were able to perceive with any one of these extended senses, you could perform magic. It would be magic, at least, to any observer not possessed of similar qualities. If you could hear radio waves crackle through the air, smell an approaching animal before it were anywhere in sight and see through walls with X-ray vision you would be credited with the abilities of a god. And you would live in a different world to the rest of us.

So now we progress a stage further still. A single drop out of a bucket of water can be home to millions of microscopic organisms. To them, the drop of water is their world; the bucket, their universe. These organisms exist around us, with us, but they do not see the world that we see. They do not recognise what would appear to us as solid barriers, as they pass through them unhindered. Their daily affairs are wholly contained within their drop of water, and they would not register (nor arguably care about) the politics, mortgages, romances and shopping excursions which, to us, appear so important.

Existence outside of the bucket may be as inconceivable to the microscopic organisms as existence outside of the known universe is to us. Everything we know of may be a drop of water in a universe of which we are totally unaware. And for all we know, these universes within universes may go on extending in either direction like an eternally replicating Russian doll. Ultimately, is any one more important than any other? The world as we know it could completely collapse into dust without ever encroaching upon the drop of water, just as the entirety of the "macro-universe" could disintegrate, transform and recreate without us raising an eyebrow. We may speculate on what wonders there are to behold in these "other universes", but at the same time we see this line of thought is misleading when we remember that these are not *other* universes, but all this one – it's just a matter of scale. With the self-contained nature of these universes, with all our hopes and fears bound to a single layer of the onion, it begs the question: does it matter which one of these layers we reside in?

Yet it is not even a question of scale, as we can peer into these alternate universes with microscopes and telescopes without gaining any appreciation of what existence is like in that realm. One may go on a package holiday and traipse around all the sight-seeing tours without learning a thing about the country being visited. One has to live as a local for that. It is a question of viewpoint. What part of the whole great show are we choosing to view, and from where are we choosing to view it? And through what colour spectacles?

Now that we seem journey-bound on a tour of the metaphysical, let's go another couple of stages further, or perhaps off to the side, depending on your viewpoint.

Chapter 10: The Tenth Not

Imagine for a moment that your whole life – your birth, upbringing, career, family activities, retirement and ultimate demise – occurred in the space of 24 hours. This is the life of the Mayfly (although I'm not sure what careers they pursue or whether they get to retire). Some varieties only live for several hours. This would constitute an intolerably brief existence for us, but does it appear so to the Mayfly? No doubt they consider this period adequate for a fulfilling lifetime of adventure. They have a different perception of the passage of time.

The tree people of the *Lord of the Rings*, the *Ents*, take an infuriatingly long time to say anything – particularly in their native tongue. Yet for these creatures, many centuries in age, they would not consider their conversation to be slow, as it is not disproportionate to their life cycles.

It is not straightforward to ascertain what speed we perceive the world around us. The industry standard for film makers is a 24Hz frame rate, and these 24 pictures per second generally appear to us as a smooth flow of imagery consistent with our perception of reality. But estimates of what we are actually capable of perceiving vary wildly – anywhere from 7Hz to well over 100Hz depending on whether we are talking about motion detection, flash imagery, peripheral versus foveal vision, plus other factors such as light intensity. The point is that there is a limit, which in some circumstances is not particularly high, beyond which any difference is, for us, undetectable.

The significance of this has been brought to life with the advent of ultra slow motion video replays, which are capable of transforming phenomena so common place as to be mundane, like a pebble dropping into water or an igniting match, into something quite spectacular. We are constantly surrounded by beautiful and captivating imagery that just goes by too rapidly for us to catch.

145

I recall seeing a video made by some folks who went around chasing tornados to capture them on film – a hazardous occupation indeed. Whilst editing their close-up footage, they reduced a section down to slow motion and discovered something astonishing and quite unexpected. There were what could best be described as glowing strips of light, perhaps several yards long, snaking around and diving through the centre of the tornado at alarming speed (even in slow motion), giving the impression of a life form unlike anything known to science. They were too quick to be visible when played back at normal speed, so the group went back to check their earlier videos of other tornados and observed a similar phenomenon on some of this footage, when replayed in slow motion. Perhaps there is a perfectly rational explanation for this manifestation. Perhaps it was an anomaly with the camera, or perhaps the whole thing was a hoax. If that be the case it was an extremely convincing one, as this was on analogue film before the days of Photoshop.

Whether or not we choose to accept the validity of the tornado light worms, the *possibility* of such phenomena is entirely plausible. We don't have ultra slow motion footage for even a tiny fraction of what goes on in the world, and with the inexorable march of time as we know it, hour after hour, day after day, even if we had we would not have the time to examine it all. Makes one wonder how much passes by us on a daily basis that we simply don't see. And this is only taking vision into account. I will allow the reader to extrapolate what may be inferred for the other senses.

Returning to a more sedate pace for the moment, let us reconsider the longevity of a tree – something like a sturdy pine branching out over the course of a thousand years. Should we afford the tree a degree of consciousness, the passage of the seasons in tree-time probably equates to our passage of night and day. The awareness and frame rate perception of the pine is likely to be such that it wouldn't even notice a hiker walking along beside it. One could head out to the forest in the summer months and build a log cabin in the pine's vicinity, and upon first noticing it, the tree may well be startled – believing the cabin to have just appeared out of nowhere.

Moving out to the scope of the planet, there is the Gaia Hypothesis, which encourages a view of the Earth as a self-regulating system, whereby organic and inorganic elements interact to produce conditions conducive to the continuation of life on the planet. On the one hand, atmospheric conditions and temperature are effected by biological life, and conversely on the other, the evolution of species are effected by their environmental conditions, and these factors combine to find equilibriums. Such an equilibrium may produce environments outside suitable thresholds for some species, but ultimately they will support the best interests of life as a whole. What such a view does is encourage us to look upon certain atmospheric and climatic manifestations, most notably the much-touted idea of "global warming", as part of a natural process of rebalancing to a new equilibrium, the cycles of which extending over lengthier periods than we are accustomed to considering. We are not going to speculate on the truth or otherwise of this theory, but we can take some of the ideas and explore some concepts that arise, hopefully stretching the anthropomorphism a little further by endowing the Earth with a consciousness.

Imagine the Earth were aware, in some fashion, of the course of its extensive history. The rise and fall of civilisations would be barely noticed – hardly making a mark in the calender. Species would come and go without a flicker of recognition. But perhaps our world does take note of cyclical changes, like a rhythmic rise and fall of temperatures, that are of the same order of magnitude for it as the rhythmic cycle of our breath or the beating of our hearts. Accurate records of weather patterns have only been kept for the last hundred years or so, and although we can make educated guesses we don't really know what climatic conditions were like stretching back over the millennia. Allan & Delair, for example, put forward a convincing case to suggest that the so-called "ice ages" never happened. They showed how all the evidence commonly presented to support their existence can be more easily explained by other phenomena, such as a single cataclysmic event. What we term as "continental drift" may be part of a choreographed dance around the surface of the planet, endlessly encircling in periodic patterns that we shall never be able to witness. We simply have no means of observation over such expanses of time, and therefore have no real knowledge of what goes on. We are a fly on the windscreen, pretending we know everything about the history of the car upon which we are sat.

I shall not bother to extend the discussion to astronomical distances and time spans as the point should be clear: speed alone forever puts events out of our reach, whether they be too fast or too slow. The unfolding of time as we experience it has an influential hold over our conception of reality.

Without wishing to disorientate you, let us now travel back to the other extreme of scale, past the microorganisms and into the realm of atoms, where proton and neutron nuclei are encircled by orbiting electrons. Modern discoveries suggest that this is probably not an accurate picture of the subatomic world, but it will suffice for our purposes.

Similar to when we see models of the solar system that have over-sized planets which do not accurately reflect the vastness of the distances between them, so it is with most diagrams and models of atoms. The space between all those electrons and the nucleus in ratio to the size of the particles is so great that if all the space were taken away and the particles compacted together the Earth would be reduced to the size of a garden pea. If that were not surprising enough, the "particles" themselves do not have a solid form as such, and are more accurately described as patterns of energy. Mystics have long asserted that the physical universe is an illusion, and at this level we would have grounds for considering it so. The objects which appear solid to us do so only because we are accustomed to viewing these patterns of energy, at these spacings, as being solid. We only feel them to be solid because of the polarity of charge which repels these patterns of energy away from each other. Were we not "tuned in" to visualising these patterns of energy and not subject to its forces, the universe as we know it would wink out of existence and we would pass through it unnoticed.

Is this the only kind of energy? We don't know. This is just what we can detect. From the discussion of our sense perceptions above, we know that we only perceive within a certain range, a certain band of frequencies. The possibility of other kinds of subatomic energies existing in all that empty space between the particles gives rise to the possibility of other types of solidity, just out of phase with our own, as undetected to us as we are to it.

There may be parallel universes existing right on top of us, around us, through us, occupying the same space, only tuned into a slightly different wavelength than our "reality". And this is without even getting into a discussion on dimensions higher than the three in which we regularly reside. Just as the two-dimensional worm is incapable of comprehending the pole that he has run into[16], many of the anomalies of our world which have the best minds scratching their heads may simply be evidence of four-dimensional poles. Or fifth, sixth or seventh dimensional ones. Mathematicians and physicists are working with abstractions in higher and higher numbers of dimensions and various models have been proposed to help visualise them – fascinating work and well worth exploring. In light of *String*

---

16 Reference being made here to the concept of a flat, two-dimensional worm existing on a flat, two-dimensional plane, and the idea that if a three-dimensional pole were standing on the flat plane, the worm, having run into it, would be unable to conceive of the pole that he has just struck, as it is outside of its plane of reality.

Theory, many physicists currently believe we live in a ten-dimensional universe. I am not, however, trying to assert that there is any truth in the Sci-fi movie you watched last weekend about the pan-dimensional aliens about to overthrow our world. This is just speculation to provide some viewpoints on viewpoints.

Therefore, we have the extended sense perceptions of the world, the micro and macro universes, the time streams, the parallel realities and the higher dimensions, all existing in the same space. Or do they? Let's change tack slightly and come at this from a different angle.

So now back to your personal viewpoint – your point from which you view. You may feel that this is fixed, rigid, inescapably the panorama extending from the centre of your head. But now think about the first school that you went to, or any school. If that doesn't come to you, a house you used to live in, or failing this, a place you visited recently. Got one? Do you have a picture of it? Can you see it in your "mind's eye"? OK, now where are you viewing *that* from? Before jumping to the knee-jerk response of "in my head", take some time to really examine it. What *is* that space in which the picture is constructed?

Now consider what happens when you go to sleep at night and begin to dream. For those of you who believe you don't dream, be aware that this is highly unlikely. The truth is that you don't remember them. Humans undergo cycles of deep sleep and lengthening periods of REM throughout the night. There is an amnesia barrier which affects most of us, to a greater or lesser degree, but seldom do we meet an individual who has no concept at all of ever having dreamt.

Recall if you can a moment from a dream you have experienced. Try to pick a pleasant one – there's no need to unnecessarily indulge in anything uncomfortable. Step into the reality of that dream world for a minute and take a look around. There is a world there, right? A full,

3D, multi-coloured, surround-sound, 360 degree panoramic vista. Where are you viewing *that* from? Surely, the dimensions of your skull are unreasonably constrictive to encompass the vast expanse of this parallel universe. If you do subscribe to the extreme materialist view of all such manifestations being a projection of the brain, then what space is your brain projecting into? There is no such space in your skull. If you believe your dreaming reality is a tiny projection confined to the inches of your brain tissue, then you may belong to the school of philosophy which argues that all of our everyday reality is likewise a projection that only really exists in our heads, because by this line of reasoning you have no more evidence of the reality of this world than you do of the dream world. I would ask these people, how then, do you know that you have a head? You would be forced to conclude that you are dreaming that you have a brain. We may as well all be the butterflies dreaming of the men[17].

Getting back on track, it is possible to gain a greater reality on the dream world by becoming conscious of the fact that one is dreaming whilst one is in the dream. Such an experience is known as a *Lucid Dream*. There are various techniques for inducing lucidity in one's dream states, generally centred upon breaking down the aforementioned amnesia barrier. Alcohol and other drugs are best avoided, as they will generally dull such awareness.

Anyone who has experienced the sensation, especially if they have taken the time to try and explore the nature of the lucid dream world, will testify that it appears to the senses every bit as real as the waking

---

17 Reference to quote from the Taoist text of Zhuangzi "Once upon a time, I dreamt I was a butterfly, fluttering hither and thither, to all intents and purposes a butterfly. I was conscious only of my happiness as a butterfly, unaware that I was myself. Soon I awaked, and there I was, veritably myself again. Now I do not know whether I was then a man dreaming I was a butterfly, or whether I am now a butterfly, dreaming I am a man."

151

world – at times even *hyper*-real. One can see, hear, touch and smell in the same manner in which we are accustomed, however pain is often altered or entirely absent. Physical universe laws are subject to bending and even breaking. In all, it is a world not dissimilar to our daily lives, but played by different rules.

When one is only dimly aware of dreams it is easy to pass off the phenomenon as a curious mental triviality. Although, when one takes conscious control, or even passively, but consciously, observes this realm, the staggering complexity, lifelike experience and just sheer *there*-ness of it all becomes difficult to ignore. One naturally begins to question the nature of *both* realities – with the "dream" and the "waking" realm increasingly blurring in distinction.

If we are to claim that the space which we perceive around us in our daily activities is real, then we shall have to concede that the space in which we roam through our nightly adventures is also, in its own right, real. Whether we afford it the same status or not, that space is observably there, is observably present, and is available for us to use and explore as space.

So where does it exist? Is it running parallel to our conventional world, through it, or does it exist somewhere else? Is it a different kind of space? Perhaps composed of a different kind of energy? Although we may be able to influence the dream world, to a greater or lesser degree, there are also occurrences which suggest contribution by more than one consciousness. The dream world could be a solo creation, it could be the work of many, or it could be either at different times. Does our waking world influence the dream world? Undoubtedly. Does the dream world influence our waking reality? Most certainly.

OK, I sense the mounting exasperation: "all very interesting" I hear you cry, "but what does any of this have to do with art?" Well, let us consider some implications of viewpoint with relation to the creation and appreciation of art. An immediately recognisable characteristic of art is the shifting of viewpoint. We are caused to see something in a new light, given a fresh perspective, taken out of our current state or surroundings and directed to others. This is, however, not specialised enough to capture the particular significance of the artistic experience. The warning sign of "BULL IN FIELD" may alter our viewpoint of a merry jaunt across the meadow, but we would scarcely call it art. Any informative or instructional material can give one a fresh perspective.

An experience often commented upon with regards to art is of being "transported" – taken "to another place". But what is this "other place" of which they speak? Within the concepts we have been discussing, we have a potential framework with which to understand these places and spaces. The artist invites you into a world, where you are not a mere spectator, but a participant. This understanding helps us to realign some of the concepts explored earlier:

- Entertainment generally invites one to be a spectator.
- A communication informs us of some part of a viewpoint.
- A work directed at making a statement is attempting to give you a viewpoint whole cloth, but, as with communication, does not entice you to create one.

The significance of this last point is not a trivial one, and warrants further explanation.

The physical universe is not capable of holding a viewpoint, so is not capable of co-creation. Only life is bestowed with such powers. When asleep, you are capable of creating an entire dream world (assuming it is only yourself who are creating it), and so too, when reading a work of literature, with the author as your accomplice, you

153

are capable of creating an entire world in mental pictures to accompany the tale.

Is this world any less real? Can this generated world influence the "normal" world in which you live? Indeed it can – it can be incredibly powerful. If we were to consign the world of mental pictures that we wander through whilst reading a book to simply "imagination", and thus consider it somehow unreal or unimportant, then we should have great difficulty in explaining how the world around us came about. After all, the scientific discoveries and inventions upon which our civilisations are built were formed in this space. It is the incubator of the philosophical thoughts spoken of in the introduction which have shaped our cultures. We all create and use this space to visualise concepts and resolve problems. If we are to disregard it, we should have to conclude that one's thoughts do not influence one's actions – a clearly absurd statement.

Hallucination, however it be induced (drug, fear, insanity, sleep/food deprivation, infatuation, torture/pain, hyperactivity/over-exhilaration, jealousy), could be seen as the adoption of a different viewpoint. These are not encouraged, by the way, as they are generally an unhealthy method of changing viewpoint. In our society we consider a person mad if they consistently view a different space to ours, or from a different perspective.

In a dream, it is easier for us to shift from one viewpoint to another. One minute we are playing one character in the panoply, the next we may occupy another. The landscape may transform at the sweep of a hand. Have you ever marvelled at your capacity to produce such wondrous effects? Hollywood would spend millions to create a single scene the like of which you can conjure into existence in the wink of an eye, and with far greater realism.

It is interesting to note that our reactions to situations in a dream differ markedly than we would expect, were we to be faced with a similar situation in waking life. The most perplexing, harrowing or just plain outrageous scenarios can be met with equanimity, as if they were the routine events of the day. "OK, so I can breathe underwater now and I'm talking to an enormous sea monster about the weather – so what?" That particular space, from that particular viewpoint, does not have all the associations, past conclusions and fused matrices that serve to produce our "normal" reactions. That's the baggage that we carry with us when we occupy our everyday viewpoint.

There's nothing necessarily wrong with this. We've built up a mental network of ideas to help us understand and deal with the world. Yet the associations needed by an ant to get through its average day bear no relation to the ones you or I may employ as a human, and to that degree they are *irrelevant* to us. But they are relevant to the ant – he is occupying that viewpoint.

So through art we are transported to another place, or caused to create another viewpoint, from where we are freed of the fixed associations which cause us to see things in a certain way. This is why so many people experience catharsis and consolation through art.

The act of creation is the adoption of a viewpoint – all else springs from this point. Although in the case of art we are not talking of merely adopting another viewpoint, but quite literally creating one. Art is not merely creative; it is that which inspires creation. It opens up a being's inherent ability to create viewpoints. To understand the broader scope and further reaching implications of this statement we need to complete our journey by examining the final *not*.

Eleven Things That Art is Not

Chapter 11

The Eleventh *Not*

"There is not a single true work of art that has not in the end added to the inner freedom of each person who has known and loved it."

(Albert Camus)

Life is what you live every day. It is putting the washing out to dry, picking up the kids, moaning about your boss, going out for a curry, staying in from the rain, getting stuck in the traffic, and enjoying a breezy Sunday drive with the top down.

You have a memory to record such things. Should you feel the need for assistance you can keep photo albums, diaries, scrap books, little trinkets and ornaments on mantelpieces. These may reflect life, or at least, your life.

Many professions exist solely as a response to the environment around us. There are doctors because we have diseases and injuries. There are firemen because we have fires which need to be contained. There are mechanics because we have cars, which occasionally (or, in some unfortunate cases, regularly) break down. Take a moment to examine various other professions in this light, then consider whether the artist's role can be thus so easily determined.

Throughout history individuals have been inspired by art and incorporated it into their architecture, philosophy, fashions, lifestyles and inventions. Ergo life may, at times, reflect art. Yet, seemingly related to this phenomenon, is a popular phrase with an inherent misconception: Art reflects life. No prizes here for guessing our final *not:*

Art is *not* a reflection of life.

This is where we head into the heart of the matter concerning political statements and social commentary on the existing conditions of the world. There is a parallel with the age-old question of whether men create history, or whether they are created by it. That debate has run its course, picked up another course, run that one too, taken up the triathlon, mountaineering and the Gumball Rally[18], and gotten all the T-shirts. But whereas it seems impossible to untangle the endlessly interwoven crossovers of that intersection, we can see a clearer path toward our current goal.

Following on from the last chapter, many speak of the transportation experienced by art; the feeling of being taken to another place, exploring another realm, being given a glimpse of an alternate

---

18 The Gumball Rally is an annual 3,000 mile race which takes place on public roads, usually between prominent cities, although the venues change every year. The supercars which take part are often driven by wealthy or famous people.

reality or parallel universe. Art is not just what you see in front of you, every day – it gives you a view of something else.

> *"Before a painting one must see something other than what one knows already. Associations and significances mingle together beyond the palette."*
>
> *(Valerio Adami)*

There is minimal creation in producing an exact duplicate of the physical universe. Holiday snaps, reality TV, news reports (although some of these are wildly imaginative and misleading), and such carbon copies of life are merely trying to tell us what is there. We could glean the same information by viewing the scene for ourselves. Biographies, encyclopedia, history books, documentaries, all have their place and perform an important function. They are informing us about subjects of interest and the world around us.

But what of the wonderment in the eyes at the illusionist's moment of revelation? Art doesn't just tell us what's there; it says there could be something else, too. It dances along the line between imagination and understanding. We have intimated as much already from the creation of viewpoints discussed in the last chapter, so let's pick up the thread and see where else it might lead.

The first place we are going to look for some assistance may appear an unlikely source to many: mathematics. If the mere utterance of that word makes you want to run, screaming with horror, in the opposite direction, then please don't be alarmed. We shall be talking in general terms about the subject, not getting into technicalities. The important part is to grasp the concepts – the details, which shall be kept to a minimum, are of no great significance.

Mathematics is often misconstrued in its classification as a subject, and the way it is usually taught in schools contributes to a misunderstanding of its essential nature. It is often portrayed as a science, or as a technical subject in the bracket of engineering, computing and data analysis. That these subjects utilise maths in their calculations and experiments adds to the confusion. The branches of mathematics they use, however, such as mechanical maths or statistical maths, collectively known as *applied mathematics*, could be seen as a corruption of the true core subject (although don't ever let an applied mathematician hear you calling it that).

Pure mathematics is actually fundamentally opposed to science in its approach to knowledge, which is what lies at the heart of both. For a scientist, it is enough to show that a certain number of results are consistent and generally predictable to derive a law. There is even an acceptable margin of "experimental error" which can be allowed for. If the experiment is shown to work 98 times out of 100, you can pretty much chalk it up as a fact.

But no amount of positive examples, even ranging up into the millions or billions, will ever satisfy the mathematician of the existence of a general principal. He is concerned *only* with logical proof. It must be shown to hold irrefutably for all possible cases.

To provide an example, you may be familiar with *Prime numbers*. These are numbers which can only be divided by one and themselves, so 4 would not be a prime number, as it can be divided by 2, but 5 would be a prime number because it can only be divided by 1 and 5.

Now to pose a question: how many prime numbers are there? We might attempt to answer this question by counting them up: 2, 3, 5, 7, 11, 13, 17..., the way that a biologist might go about determining the total number of species of birds. Once we had gotten up to over a million and seen that there are still plenty of prime numbers around, we could assume that we have gathered enough evidence to suggest that this trend continues indefinitely and leave it at that. But a mathematician would not be happy at this. He would ask: "How do you know they don't dry up once you get past a billion?" Even if we used the most powerful supercomputer on Earth to calculate answers, there would always be a limit that we could not go beyond, and therefore we would always be unsure of our conclusion.

Fortunately, we don't have to go to this trouble, because this problem was solved by a Greek mathematician called Euclid well over two thousand years ago. Here is a simplified variation of the proof that he offered:

Let's assume we have a prime number, which we will call P. This could stand for any prime number. Now we are going to find a new number, which we will call N, by multiplying together all the numbers up to and including P, then adding one. So:

$1 \times 2 \times 3 \times 4 ... \times P + 1 = N$

Now, this new number N...

> ...cannot be divisible by 2 because it would leave 1 left over...
> ...cannot be divisible by 3 because it would leave 1 left over...
> ...cannot be divisible by 4 because it would leave 1 left over...
> ...cannot be divisible by P because it would leave 1 left over...

...so we are left with two options: 1) N is a prime number, or 2) N is divisible by a number larger than P, and we know that this number is also not divisible by any of the numbers up to P. In either case, we have found a new prime number which is larger than P. Therefore, no matter what prime number we choose to begin with, there will always be a larger one.

161

By these few logical steps, we have shown that there is an infinite number of primes, and by following this line of reasoning, *you* can be as sure as Euclid was of this conclusion, without having to count up to millions.

To properly understand this crucial difference between science and mathematics, and to appreciate why it is so crucial, we need to understand what these subjects are founded upon, and how they are constructed.

Science is a branch of philosophy which presupposes that we can learn about objective reality through observation of the physical universe. We shall leave aside for now the validity or otherwise of this approach from a philosophical standpoint, and acknowledge that it does at least have some workability – one need only look at the world around them for supporting evidence.

Pure Mathematics, on the other hand, is in no way concerned with the physical universe. The models, diagrams and graphs may suggest otherwise, but these are merely visual aids to help in grasping concepts which are entirely abstract. It would be a mistake to think that mathematicians spend all their time working on worldly problems. As Jerry King points out, there are tens of thousands of mathematicians worldwide producing thousands of papers at a greater rate than ever before, but they are invisible to the rest of the world – even their intellectual peers. The scientists and engineers, who see mathematics as nothing but a tool in their daily work, have no real idea what the pure mathematicians are doing.

So what does it mean to *do* mathematics? The aim of a Scientist's work is apparent – to contribute to the body of science, to the accumulated knowledge of the subject. This is continually shifting, or at least should be, as new data presents itself which questions the current beliefs or sheds new light on established facts. We cannot talk of an absolute proof in science. Old theories are discarded in favour of new, and one never knows when the next "Copernican revolution"[19] is just around the corner. Scientific theories can only ever be the best theories to fit the currently available evidence.

Mathematics does not progress in this fashion. The mathematical landscape is an abstract one which is based on certain axioms that describe its character – they are the rules by which the game must be played. Progress is made by finding new things that can be done within these rules, and that are proved to be correct because they follow, logically, from the original axioms. Given that mathematical theorems and laws are based solely on logical proof, they are not superseded, only added to. What was once true in mathematics has always been true, and will always be true.

The field of play is ever expanding, as new concepts, relationships and potentialities are introduced. But note that, unlike science which relies on observation of the physical universe for data, the mathematical realm relies on nothing but consistency with itself and the axioms upon which it was constructed. And another whole playing field could be constructed by starting with different axioms. Scientific truths are discovered; mathematical truths are created.

So a mathematician's work is the creation of mathematics in a mathematical plane of reality. And they are guided in their creations by intuition and a sense of beauty. Pure mathematics is an abstract art form. To quote Jerry King from his excellent work *The Art of Mathematics:*

---

19 The *Copernican Revolution* was named after the Polish scientist who first championed the heliocentric idea of the Earth and other planets revolving around the sun, as opposed to the widely-believed concept of a static Earth. More than simply scientific theory, it is termed a revolution due the way it shifted the world view, significantly affecting the philosophy and theology of at the time.

Eleven Things That Art is Not

> *"To do mathematics is to do research, which means to create mathematics as a poet creates poems."*

Interestingly enough, an experiment was done in America in the 1970s, whereby a group of school children were taught mathematics not in the dry conventional way, with one apple plus one apple equals two apples, but like it is from the bottom up. It was explained how the subject is created, that it exists on an abstract plane like an imaginary landscape, built upon axioms or rules by which you have to play the game, and that mathematicians create patterns, structures and concepts in this space. They attempted to impart some of the aesthetic pursuit which motivates mathematicians, excites them and keeps them returning to the subject. An overwhelming majority of that group of children went on to become mathematics professors.

To tie this in with our overall discussion we need to consider one further concept and expand on the statement made earlier that mathematical truths are created. This claim is refuted by *absolutists* who hold the idea, which stretches back at least as far as Plato, that mathematics exist independent of thought, and that any truths concerning its nature are merely discovered as a scientist discovers truths about physical reality. Numbers, shapes, etc. have a definite identity, as real as any physical object, and their characteristics are already there to be examined. This line of reasoning suggests that if a solitary person, scribbling away with his pencil one evening, comes up with a new mathematical concept, model or set of axioms, then every single truth concerning it will automatically spring into existence instantaneously, and lie there waiting for the mathematicians to latch onto them. In other words, they have an objective reality.

It becomes difficult to maintain this perspective when we consider modern mathematics which deal in abstractions so far removed from any physical plane of reality that it is virtually impossible to even think of them in those terms. The alternative perspective, which seems to embrace the direction which mathematics has increasingly taken, is that mathematical truths are created, and do not have any kind of objective reality outside of the minds of those who created or study them. They exist purely in the thought of the thinkers and nowhere else.

This perspective would seem to be supported by the philosophy of Immanuel Kant (and many Western thinkers since), who argued that pure reason is dominant only in a subjective sense, and that we can never be sure of what it tells us about objective reality, so it is of little use in that arena. Subjective space is the arena in which mathematical reason operates. 20th century Analytic Philosophy goes further, to suggest that mathematics *cannot* tell us anything about objective reality. Given that pure mathematics is entirely an abstract construct based on arbitrary laws, there is some grounding for this belief.

The problem with this perspective is that mathematics observably has many uses and parallels in the physical world around us. If it be a purely subjective phenomenon, existing only in thoughts and imaginations, then it is surprising that it would find *any* application. The proof of the pudding is in the eating, and the sciences, technical disciplines and economics have feasted heavily upon mathematics to produce the modern world.

There is a way to marry these two perspectives. We have some clues if we take a closer look at some of the applications. In particular, we will look at the curious phenomena of mathematical developments acting as a precursor to scientific discovery.

The geometry with which most people are familiar, involving shapes, angles, planes and solids, was formulated by the same Greek mathematician mentioned earlier, Euclid. It is based upon a simple set

165

of axioms which were thought to mirror the physical world, and therefore have great applicability, although the reasoning and conclusions drawn from these axioms remained consistent outside of any comparison with physical reality.

It wasn't until the early 19th century that geometry was considered to be anything other than Euclidean geometry. At this time, several other "non-Euclidean" geometries were proposed. Bernhard Riemann developed one such geometry which was totally logical and consistent, but was derived from axioms that varied considerably from Euclid's. For example, his axioms allowed for more than one straight line to be drawn between two points *(see Fig.2)*. This notion would have appeared absurd to those from earlier times, and it may appear difficult for you to accept now, but remember that we are dealing with an abstract concept, a mathematical universe which doesn't necessarily have to be consistent with the physical universe – it only needs to be consistent with itself.

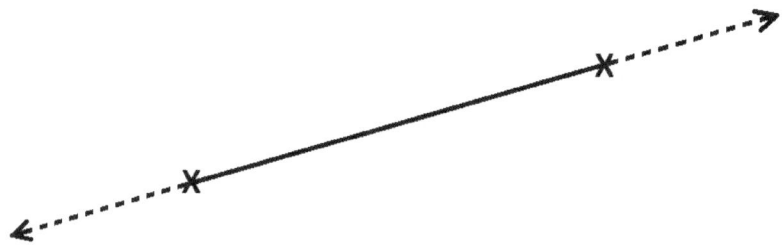

Fig.2 - According to Euclid's axioms, only one straight line can be drawn between two points

Another significant difference lay in parallel lines. Euclid's axioms contained the *Parallel Postulate,* which stated that, given a straight line and a point not on that line, there is exactly one straight line which runs through the point and is parallel to the other line *(see Fig.3)*. In Riemann's geometrical world, there is *no* such line which will run parallel.

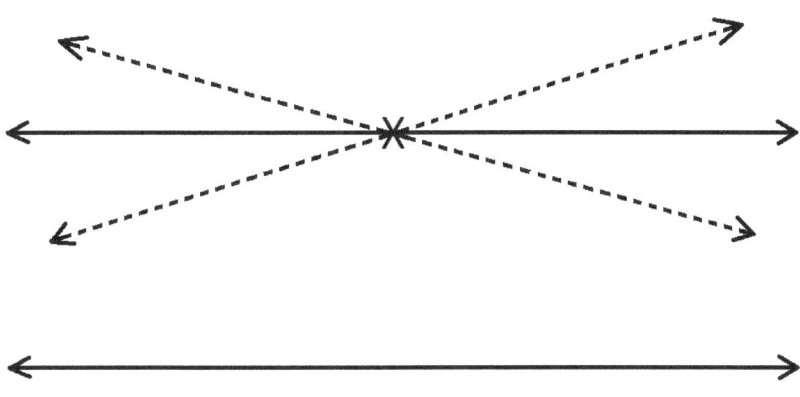

Fig.3 – Euclid's parallel postulate

Other geometries were subsequently developed, but all of these Non-Euclidean geometries were thought to have no use outside of the introspective world of the pure mathematician. That is, until the early 1900s when Einstein used them as a model for his theory of relativity. Scientists now believe that Non-Euclidean geometry actually provides us with a more accurate picture of the physical universe.

Taking another example, a branch of pure mathematics called *Matrices*, which deals with operations on large sets of numbers as though they were a single object, found use in quantum mechanics by Werner Heisenberg many years after it was developed.

A similar relationship exists for what are known as *complex numbers,* or sometimes (rather questionably) as *imaginary* numbers. Conventional wisdom in arithmetic tells us that we cannot find the square root[20] of a negative number. This is because a negative number, when squared (multiplied by itself), gives a positive result *(i.e. negative x negative = positive)*. Conversely, when we find the square root of a number, we always obtain two results – a negative and a positive. For example:

$\sqrt{9} = 3$ *and* -3

because

$3^2 = 3 \times 3 = 9$

and

$(-3)^2 = (-3) \times (-3) = 9$

But what would happen if we supposed we *could* find the square root of a negative number? Do we get a different kind of number that we haven't seen before? This notion was debated and refuted for some time until it was shown that, by assuming we could find negative square roots, we could solve some important questions in mathematics.

And thus the complex numbers came into existence. We shan't dwell on the technicalities, but out of interest, a model for thinking about these numbers was constructed by taking the conventional number line, which has all the regular numbers on it:

---

20 A number which, when multiplied by itself, gives the required value e.g. the square root of 4 is 2, because
2 x 2 = 4.

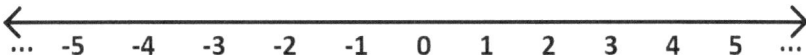

and adding an axis to make a 2D plane, rather than just a line:

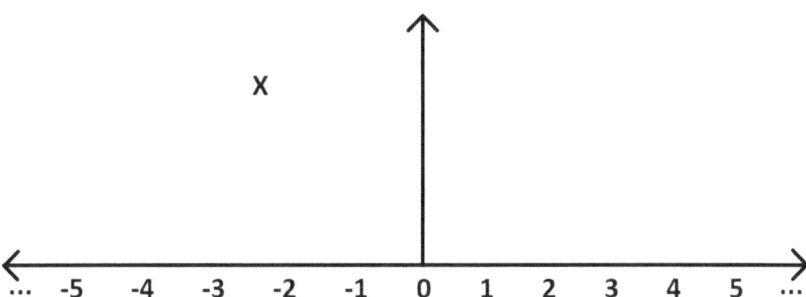

The point marked "x", as an example, would be a complex number. Once again, although they played an increasingly important role in mathematics over a couple of centuries, it seemed unlikely that complex numbers would have relevance to the everyday world. Even the mathematician has to do a metaphorical leap of faith to accept their existence. Rene Descartes originally dubbed them "imaginary" numbers as he suspected their validity to be dubious.

Despite their usefulness in solving some calculations with real numbers, the amount of direct applications of complex numbers in the physical world remained extremely limited. That is, until we entered the domain of quantum mechanics, where they form a perfect fit for describing the subatomic world.

Perhaps this is all simply coincidence. Although the proliferation of examples tends to contradict this evaluation. It brings into question which direction the line of causality is flowing. A possible resolution to the two perspectives on mathematics, as described above, could be that mathematics is *both* created subjectively, *and then* acquires an objective reality. This could be one way to go. But before we draw any definite conclusions, let us linger in the field of quantum mechanics and expand on what it can bring to the table of our discussion.

As covered in the previous chapter, the subatomic world is an intriguing place. The first thing we encounter is the *wave-particle duality*, in that protons and electrons appear as both a particle and a wave, depending upon how they are viewed. This leads to Niels Bohr's conclusion in his *Principal of Complementarity* that a complete knowledge of the phenomena requires a description of the properties of both. It was stated above that the miniature solar-system model of atoms was not really accurate, and this is where we start to break it down.

The tone produced by a well-played flute is very pure, and can approach a sine wave (a smooth, even-curved wave). Playing a single note, this is an example of a single frequency wave. Conversely, white noise is composed of many waves at a wide range of frequencies, all of equal intensity. Consequently, this confusion of sounds produces no discernable pitch. It is for this reason that percussion instruments fall into two categories: tuned and untuned. The tuned instruments, such as a xylophone, produce a wave of a recognisable frequency, so the notes of a scale can be represented – one note for each block. Whereas some drums, for example, produce multiple waves at various frequencies which result in no definite pitch. Numerous physical factors influence which waves will be produced, such as the size and shape of the drum, temperature, humidity, tension of the skin, and where and with what it is struck. In studying the puzzling behaviour of subatomic particles, physicists began to use the model of a vibrating drum as a better approximation of what they were observing.

Back in the 1700s, the great mathematician Leonard Euler produced his *wave equation*. By feeding in the various properties of a drum, this equation can be used to calculate the possible wave patterns that it will generate. There is, however, an important difference between the character of a drum and the character of an atom. In order to attempt calculations on atomic behaviour, physicists had to enter the realm of imaginary numbers. And this is where things start to get really weird.

Science, as we have said, is predicated on objective observation. A thorn in the side of this bold quest for the acquisition of knowledge is the *observer effect*. Simply put, this is the idea that one effects the thing being observed by the act of observing it, therefore precluding any truly objective observation. When we watch something we will, however slightly, influence it. There have long been proverbs supporting this idea, such as "a watched kettle never boils", but for the majority of physical experiments, the effect is negligible, as far as we can tell. The scientist can hold on to the cherished idea of the "impartial observer". Indeed, although philosophy has long been telling us that reason alone cannot penetrate objective reality, the implications of this is something that science seemed determined to ignore. It is, however, what science ran slap bang into the face of in quantum physics.

The true nature of a subatomic particle appears more like a field of potentiality than anything definite one could put one's finger on. They exist in more than one location at the same time, and at more than one frequency. They can exist for a millionth of a millionth of a second, and are constantly changing state. Physicists encourage us to drop the idea of them having an identity of their own. And here's the kicker: whatever we do to observe them changes their behaviour.

171

The goal, therefore, of quantum mechanics is to try and describe the subatomic world devoid of observations. One can see where the difficulty lies. This is the genesis of the famous *Schroedinger's Cat* analogy[21]. Prior to observation, governed solely by imaginary numbers, these probabilistic fields float in transient ethereality, all things to all men. Once spied, they cease to be described by imaginary numbers and become a string of ordinary ones. It is as if we were peering into a multi-dimensional world through a one-dimensional telescope (or, more appropriately, microscope). We don't hear the white noise, nor even a drum. All that drifts across the borderline between these worlds is the single, solitary tone of a lonely flute.

It's not difficult to see the crossover with our topic of viewpoints. But our question on the direction of flow was left open. Is it that we are viewing only a slice of reality through our one-dimensional filter, thus seeing only one facade of the potential many? Perhaps this is the origin of the *multiverse* concept, which suggests that all potential outcomes are played out on parallel planes of reality. Or, is it that we are observing some of the process by which what we know of as reality is brought into being? Is there a line of causality working not only to decide what version of reality we see around us, but to actively create and shape that very reality?

The crucial point to reiterate about the observer effect, as it presents itself in quantum mechanics, is not that we are only observing a small part of the phenomena, but that we are *interacting* with the phenomena by observing it. The "particles" (for want of a better term) actually *change state* when we take some action to view them. To

---

21 A thought experiment proposed by physicist Erwin Schroedinger to attempt to illustrate current theory on quantum mechanics in terms of everyday objects. A much simplified version of the idea is to imagine a cat in a sealed box. Without opening the box it is not known whether the cat is alive, and so until it is observed, it could be said to exist in an indeterminate state of being both dead and alive.

launch into the implications of this, I give you Max Planck, the father of quantum mechanics, as he assures us there is no matter, as such:

> "All matter originates and exists only by virtue of a force which brings the particle of an atom to vibration and holds this most minute solar system of the atom together. We must assume behind this force the existence of a conscious intelligent mind. This mind is the matrix of all matter."

Now we place the horse more firmly before the cart and see who's driving this show. Interestingly, since accepting reason's impotence to knowing objective reality, Western philosophy has followed a path of embracing contradiction and irrationality as a clearer indication of reality, should there be such a thing. We could postulate the mysterious subatomic world, with its contrary appearances of particles simultaneously existing in more than one location, to be a parallel of this chaotic, inherent nature of reality. But it is life which brings order to this chaos. We are not going to speculate on the nature of the ultimate reality, but we now know who shapes, crafts and influences the form of what we know as reality – what we interact with day to day.

Do we have any other evidence to support this claim? Plenty. Let us take the medical profession. It may surprise you to know that 43% of all drugs prescribed by doctors are actually placebos. They have no known capabilities of curing the condition or relieving symptoms, and the pharmacists are aware of this when they hand them over the counter. This is not because they secretly harbour some evil desire to be deliberately deceitful, but because they know that a large number of people will get well simply because they believe they are being treated. The phenomenon has been consistently observed over many years. The medicos may not know why it happens, but they know it to be true.

This in itself, however, is only a symptom of a wider condition.

When we look to the causes of illness we discover that 70% of them are, to greater or lesser degree, psychosomatic. A full examination of this subject is outside the scope of this book (see the bibliography for the interested reader), but it is beyond doubt that the majority of the physical ailments of which we are afflicted have come about through mental processes. For whatever reason, we do it to ourselves. This may be uncomfortable for some to accept, yet for others it is liberating. The reader shall be spared a multitude of examples (of which there are a plethora to choose from), but shall hopefully allow the author a brief indulgence in personal experience.

For the first twenty years of my lifetime I suffered from asthma. It was always there, lurking in the background, and not a day went by without the monster rearing its ugly head. At one point the doctors were concerned that the growth of my body was being restricted during its formative years due to the amount of energy I was expending on breathing. I was on several medications which I had to carry around with me everywhere, and lived in fear of them running out.

Until, that is, the day that I discovered it to be a psychosomatic condition – an idea which at first struck me as inconceivable, given how real the experience was in my daily life. And yet, on further examination and after some mental exercises, I knew it to be true. The condition cleared up literally overnight, never to return. I, for one, no longer need to be convinced of the power of our mental faculties over physical structure.

In a different, yet related field, Dr. Vladimir Poponin and his colleague Peter Gariaev have conducted experiments to observe what they call the *phantom DNA effect*, which suggests that human DNA can directly affect the physical universe. Further evidence goes on to imply that emotions, measurable as wave energy, directly affect the structure of DNA, even at a distance.

Chapter 11: The Eleventh Not

Taking a wider view than one's own physical body, have you ever known someone who was really focused on achieving a goal, dedicated towards a given path, and everything just seemed to "fall into place"? The right opportunities just coincidentally seemed to open up for them. It is as if the world moved around to accommodate their wishes. It may have happened to you, on a small or large scale. Perhaps you just decided you really needed to get that new car, and somehow you were sure it was going to happen, but you had no conceivable way of obtaining it. Then, out of the blue, the showroom has a sale on, and the exact sum of money you needed falls into your lap – an unexpected tax rebate, an inheritance from a distant relative, etc. This kind of phenomena goes on with alarming frequency. Just by consistently holding something in the mind it can be brought into existence.

But alas, we are tipping the iceberg on another subject which could easily get us lost in a deep blue ocean, so we need to get back on track. Surely, we may ask, the world is solid and real enough, it is governed by physical laws that are all known and tabulated, and science has got all this taped, right?

Unfortunately not. Michael Brooks makes it clear in his book *13 Things That Don't Make Sense*, that the world of science continues to be plagued by "anomalies" which defy any known explanation. And the implications of these anomalies reach right down to the core of the sciences and threaten everything we think we know. In *The Science Delusion*, Rupert Sheldrake outlines ten dogmas of modern science which, despite being unsupported by the available evidence, are fervently held onto and are therefore holding back the progress of research, discovery and knowledge. These are not trifling affairs. We are talking about some of the most major tenets of science. One of them surrounds consciousness, or more specifically, the scientific establishment's insistence that there isn't any.

The doctrine of *Materialism* – that all is composed of matter, devoid of consciousness – leaves far too many phenomena unexplained to be plausible. Just the utterly astronomical odds against any kind of organised forms, let alone life forms, occurring out of pure random chance makes the proposition unthinkable. It simply doesn't fit the picture of what we see around us every day. Yet it is within this framework that the main body of science has tried to squeeze its results since the late 1800s, no matter how far outside of it they fall. Contemporary science seems to have all but forgotten that it has wholeheartedly adopted this philosophical standpoint, as it is now accepted without inspection.

Let it be said here, I am in no way "anti-science" – it is an invaluable branch of philosophy. Nor, it must be said, is Sheldrake – himself a lifelong scientist with over eighty published papers to his name, who frequently lectures at universities across the world. He just wants to see the sciences freed of the "dogmatic ideology, fear-based conformity and institutional inertia" to which they have "lost most of their vigour, vitality and curiosity". There are many scientists doing fantastic work who struggle to gain acceptance from the orthodoxy. Funding comes largely from establishments with a vested interest in furthering a particular line of research, such as pharmaceutical companies or other large industries. New ideas more often meet scorn or ridicule than they do acceptance. Popular theories follow fads and fashions rather than being subjected to a critical eye. It would appear that the mainstream of science has befallen some of the same pitfalls as the mainstream of the arts.

Refocusing on theories for the moment, let us remember that a theory is never conclusively proven in science. It can only ever be the best current theory to fit the available evidence. This is true even of the so-called "laws". One of these laws, taken up by Sheldrake, amongst others, is the conservation of energy – the idea that the total amount of matter and energy never varies, it only changes form. Accepting this as an invariable truth is one of the factors that has led modern Physics to the baffling conclusion that 96% of the universe is missing, and that the unaccounted for majority must be composed of a kind of matter or energy that nobody has ever observed or measured on any instrument anywhere. If you think science has got it all covered, look no further than this to be disabused of the idea. The conservation of energy "law" also has importance for our line of enquiry, as the creation of viewpoints suggests that there may be a creation of energy, in some form.

Another mainstay which needs to be brought into question are the "constants". There are certain values, such as the Gravitational constant and the speed of light, which are held to be unchanging since the dawn of time, and upon which many of the laws of science (physics in particular) are reliant. Although, there's no actual reason why they should be constant, and there is sufficient evidence mounting to suggest that many of them are not. This is unnerving for a lot of physicists, and many of them don't want to go anywhere near it. As the universe starts to appear less fixed, regular and predictable, their mental walls start to creak and threaten to come tumbling down.

But still, the theories, laws and formulas have served us well. For all practical purposes in the everyday world they seem to work, and our general experience of the universe is fairly constant. We are therefore led to ask, if we are to believe that consciousness can manipulate, and indeed is the senior partner over, physical structure and appearances, how come we see so much uniformity in our universe? Our engineers and technicians rely on it being so, and the proof of their calculations are all around us in the structures they create. Seems pretty real and solid to me. And it doesn't matter how much I think I can fly, if I jump off the top of that tall building, there's only going to be one outcome.

True enough. But let's consider an analogy. Say you wanted to walk across a long, narrow bridge to get to the other side. If you were the only person on the bridge, this would be simple – you could do exactly as you pleased. If there were several people with you then the company might spur you on and make the journey more pleasant, and you could all come and go to your hearts content. A thousand people accompanying you would probably carry you along the way, like it or not.

Now let's say you were walking along the bridge, on your own, and there was a crowd of twenty people coming in the opposite direction. This would pose a little difficulty to your progress. Chances are you would still make it across OK, but it would require some negotiation. You may be held up for a while to let people pass, and may even become convinced you are going in the wrong direction and turn to join them.

For our final scenario, you now have a million people charging headlong in the opposite direction, straight at you, along this narrow bridge. Regardless of how determined you are to get to the other side, you're not going to make it. You'll either be swept back the other way or be trampled underfoot.

There are a lot of us on this planet. Life creates order; more life creates more order. As the tracks of mental associations become well trodden, the reality becomes solidified. The inevitability that the view out of your window will look the same every morning, that what goes up must come down, that night follows day, and that there will always be politicians and wars, exists simply because we all agree that it is so.

Imagine for a moment having a dream, perhaps a lucid dream, in which you meet another person, and possibly even discuss the fact that you are both dreaming. Upon awakening, you see this same person and you are both acutely aware that you shared the same dream the previous night.

This experience has happened to your author. You may have had a similar experience yourself. Of the many questions that arise from such a phenomenon, let us ask this: who's dream was it? It was clearly not my subjective reality, as it was shared by the other person. By the same token, it was not theirs. There is the third possibility, that this dream world had an independent objective reality, of which both my friend and I were visitors. But this doesn't seem altogether satisfactory either, due to the degree to which I was able to shape and affect this seemingly personal world. In fact, the scene in which we met was similar in terms of content, but varied in terms of specific visual interpretation. We both, however, concurred on what we had spoken of and what took place.

The most sensible conclusion, following our train of investigation, is that this space, this viewpoint, was the combined product of my friend and I – of our consciousness (disregarding for convenience the possibility of other minor influences by other bit-part players or other forms of life). It was more malleable and personal to us than the physical waking world, as it was created by only us two, yet it shared common elements for the same reason. For that period of time we created the space to share that experience.

This example alone should convince us that we need to dissolve the ideas of the subjective and objective, as it doesn't make sense to think of such things in these terms. We cannot consider one without the other. But we can consider the interactions. There is a process going on here – one in which things are brought into being.

This reversal of causality, as it may appear to some, shouldn't be unfathomable to the scientific mind. One of the most interesting features of science is the question of where the hypotheses come from. Here, scientists begin to sound mystical in their explanations of intuitions, moments of insight and flashes of inspiration which have given birth to their creative theories. The commonly forwarded impression of science is of a cold, objective observation of physical manifestations, from which a general rule is obtained. This can happen, but it is not the way that science generally tends to progress. The great advances usually occur the other way round: the ideas form first in the minds of the scientist, the theories are formulated, then a search is conducted in the physical universe to find evidence to support the theory. Popular theories obtain a lot of agreement, and so the whole process is strengthened. Then what you look for hard enough, you will inevitably find.

Linking this back in, there is an extension to the tale of complex numbers. The mathematician mentioned earlier with regard to his non-Euclidean geometry, Bernhard Riemann, is perhaps most famous for his work in another area, number theory, where he proposed the "Riemann Hypothesis". This involves complex numbers, but enters a couple more layers of abstraction and complexity beyond, so we shan't dwell on the details. The proof of this hypothesis remains an unsolved problem and, due to its importance, is probably the most sought-after target in mathematics. By the way, there's a million dollar prize up for grabs if you can crack this one. Although, I wouldn't get too hopeful, as some of the greatest minds have been banging their heads against it for well over a century.

And this is the curious point. This problem has received a terrific amount of attention over a sustained period. In attempts to solve it, countless possibilities have been explored, resulting in whole new bodies of mathematics springing up around it, inching towards a greater understanding of what makes it tick. One of these bodies of data, which dealt with the behaviour of extremely remote examples of the hypothesis calculated by a supercomputer, was found to precisely mirror observed behaviour in an equally remote field – physicists attempting to map large and complex atoms which were virtually impossible to calculate. There was no prior suggestion that the two would be in any way related, and the discovery only came about over a "chance" discussion during a tea break between two people working in their respective disciplines (the more one examines coincidences, the less coincidental they appear to be). Each was as flabbergasted as the other to find, not least that they had anything in common at all, but that their results matched perfectly.

Putting this back into the context of viewpoints, when mathematicians create abstractions, they are literally creating space. For some time now, mathematicians have been working with geometry in 4-Dimensional space, and have come up with all kinds of visualisations to help grasp this concept. Guess what? Yep, they are now highlighting a number of physical world "anomalies" that may be indications of 4D objects passing through our 3D perception of space. Who knows, at some point down the track, we may all be living in a 4D universe.

If you can conceive of that viewpoint, if you can create that viewpoint, then you can create that space. The more assuredly you create it, the greater reality it will obtain for you. You *have* that space. If others help to create this viewpoint and this space, then it will obtain a reality for you all.

And this is where the artist comes to the foreground. It was said at the top that it is the ideas which build a civilisation and shape a culture. But who provides the inspiration for the ideas? Who helps to unlock the creative potential of the philosopher, scientist, technician? The great artist is not only a master of motivating the creation of viewpoints, he also has great influence over channelling the direction and character of those viewpoints thus created.

Art, therefore, *cannot* be divorced from truth, as it comes before truth. It is a *creator* of truths. This is the proper relationship restored. And art is therefore not a reflection of life, but life may be a reflection of art. With this understanding we can realign the assertion about the

181

hierarchy of philosophical disciplines. Specifically, we must place aesthetics senior to politics, as aesthetics co-exists with metaphysics and epistemology, and cannot be subordinate to them.

There is much evidence that this was better understood in days gone by. The ancient Greeks are known by us as philosophers and scientists, yet they were known to themselves as musicians and artists. This was every bit as important to them, to the point that they did not see a distinction between the disciplines.

The artworks of spiritual traditions through the ages have provided focal points with which to align the conscious attention of whole populations. This echoes through to our time in the tribal rituals and artistic expressions of so-called "primitive" peoples. Mention was made in the introduction about the ancient Chinese culture prescribing certain musical scales for certain times of the day, and thereby holding the society together under a unified harmony. The ancient Sumerian and Babylonian civilisations had a highly sophisticated concept of harmony which was intimately associated with their cosmology, mathematics and religion.

The role played by vibration and sound frequency has many varied implications and interpretations. A metal plate covered with sand can be vibrated at different frequencies to produce different notes, and at each one the sand will form unique patterns on the surface of the plate. This was first demonstrated by Ernst Chladni in the eighteenth century by using a violin bow against the side of the plate. Picturing the metal plate as the surface of a drum gives us a parallel with the analogy of the subatomic particle.

As the frequencies are increased, higher than that obtainable by a violin bow, more intricate and beautiful patterns are produced. What is fascinating, is that these same patterns are found inscribed in ancient monuments and megalithic sites right across the globe. There are an amazing number of unifying threads running through these mysterious feats of ancient engineering. This has, however, been extensively written of elsewhere (see the Bibliography for some suggestions), so we shall not pursue it further.

Although, a word should be said about the untapped potential of sound and resonant frequencies. Given the vibrational frequencies found in the subatomic realm, the significance placed by the ancients in this area is especially intriguing. There are reports in some inscriptions of objects being moved by sound. With the presence of massive stone blocks ranging up to over a thousand tonnes in weight, slotted inch-perfect into place in these monuments, it is clear they were in possession of a different kind of technology. There is not a crane on Earth today which could lift such a weight.

Modern discoveries have seen the development of fire extinguishers which nullify roaring flames in seconds using sound frequency alone. Back in the 1930s, the microbiologist and inventor Royal Rife found that viruses respond to a particular frequency, and by using this frequency many diseases can be cured, including cancer. This work was largely ignored, however some similar discoveries have been made by more recent researchers, suggesting that we are only just beginning to realise (or just starting to recover) the potentialities in this field.

So do we wish to create harmony, or discord? The model of the artist getting people to resonate together is metaphorical in one sense, and quite literal in another. It starts to become clear why the Chinese and Indian cultures of old were so keen to preserve their musical structures, and why Plato and Aristotle voiced concerns over new musics in theirs. We can understand the statement from Lenin when he said, closer to our time: "The quickest and most effective way to undermine any society is through its music".

When someone creates some wonderful mathematics, the beauty lies not in what they have precisely communicated, but in the possibilities that are suggested by it. A simply stated equation which implies all manner of variations and meanings is extremely powerful. This is what opens the creative window in the minds of others. The artist is the piper who leads his enchanted followers into the creation of a dream.

Inevitably, we are led to questions about where the whole universe came from, for what purpose, etc. These questions are clearly for another book – one which I do not feel I have the capacity to write. But there is no question that you are affecting the universe, whether you realise it or not. You have a part to play in the creation of the world.

Don't be fooled by the specious modern fashion of Materialism – that which denounces your capabilities, that which says there is no purpose to anything, that thoughts exist only in brains which are themselves only chemicals that have been randomly thrown together. It is this idea which stops you from appreciating what you really are. It is this idea which confines the artist to the role of the court jester.

So I restate: art is not merely creative; it is that which inspires creation.

We now have a better idea of what is meant by the creation of a viewpoint. It is not proclaiming a message to the world like so many billboards passing uninspected before our eyes. Art doesn't simply present you with a viewpoint, a quaint little picture for you to look at and say "oh yes, very nice dear, very pretty". It enjoins you to produce a new viewpoint, and in doing so you are literally creating the future, creating a reality. Art provides the impetus for beings to use their inherent powers of creation along a given line. When that which has been created falls out of the attention of life, it falls back into disorder.

Chapter 11: The Eleventh Not

As an artist, you are powerful beyond your greatest hopes and fears. If you have any doubt about this just think about the majestic universe you are able to create whole cloth every time you go to sleep at night. It may cause you to think twice about what you choose to put out into the world. What kind of a world would you like to live in? Into what sort of a future might we project ourselves? Should you wish to try and portray how terrible everything is, then you may be a bigger part of the problem than you realise. Yet your capacity for creation is infinitely stronger than your capacity for destruction. If this is at all daunting, I shall leave you with the inspirational words of Marianne Williamson:

> *"Our deepest fear is not that we are inadequate. Our deepest fear is that we are powerful beyond measure. It is our light, not our darkness that most frightens us. We ask ourselves, who am I to be brilliant, gorgeous, talented and fabulous? Actually, who are you not to be? You are a child of God. Your playing small doesn't serve the world. There is nothing enlightening about shrinking so that people won't feel insecure around you. We are all meant to shine... ...and as we let our light shine, we unconsciously give other people permission to do the same. As we are liberated from our own fear, our presence automatically liberates others."*

Eleven Things That Art is Not

Summary

We are now able to readdress Duchamp's *fountain*. The effect it had, and one of the supposed intentions behind it, was to question what we consider to be art by testing the fringes and challenging what should be included under it's banner – seeing what could be squeezed into view when one squints and looks out of the corner of one's eye in a murky, misleading twilight. But surely this is the wrong line of approach. If one wanted to define a tree, you wouldn't start in by looking at a broom handle and trying to see if you could call it a tree, then attempting to define the broom handle. You would examine the most perfect, thunderous oak, and try to determine from this what are all the prominent qualities that are characteristically tree-like. Examine the best example you can find to discover its purposes, make-up, potentials; don't examine a broom handle stuck in mud. The focus is in the wrong direction. We're back to Freud studying the abnormalities; we need to study the excellences.

This is the purpose behind the examination of your Prime Experience, as this is the direction whereby we are likely to learn something useful. When confronted with a genuine artistic experience, you *know* about it. If you have to question whether it is art, you've probably got your answer.

Regardless, as has been shown from all we've covered, the question itself is misplaced. It implies that a static phenomenon can be once labelled as art, and from that moment on it always will be. But this is falling back into the trap of the subject/object duality. Art is *not* a possession. There is a dynamic process going on. There is the artistic *experience*. At the moment where you are asking "is this art?" or "is that art?", for sure, there is no art taking place.

One practical use of separating out these *nots*, is to help realign us in our own, personal appreciation of art, or potential art. When you come to view a painting, refrain from getting your camera out, or chatting to your friend, putting your headphones on, or anything else. Try to be quiet, still. Really *look* at it. If any judgemental thoughts come into your head, suppress them, gently. No marks out of ten. Don't start trying to figure out the deep or hidden meaning behind it. Just experience it. Give it time. If it takes you somewhere, let it take you, and see if you like it, or if you find it interesting.

It's also worth considering the other side of the equation for a moment. If you have produced a work of art and someone else has appreciated it, then no matter what your feelings may be about it, be glad that they have gotten something from it. Don't spoil it by picking out all the errors you made, saying how disappointed you were with it and that you weren't up to your usual standard. Let them have what they got out of it. They may have been inspired in ways that you never intended, and been taken to places that you never imagined, but thus is the power of art. Be happy that this happens – you've done a valuable job.

OK, so we've looked at the *nots*. There may be others (there have already been a few bonus ones thrown in, for those of you paying attention). As we have walked through this disrobing you may have noticed other garments hanging by their threads; incongruent and unwarranted adornments disguising the purity of form beneath. Perhaps now we have only revealed an inner layer, continuing to shroud our quarry in mystery.

We've learned a bit about what it is not. So what *is* it?

Is it practical, or even possible to extricate art entirely from the categories delineated above? Will this Emperor ever be free of his clothes? Possibly not. But what are the benefits in trying or moving towards it? Moreover, what are the dangers of leaving things to continue as they are? So what if we refer to a well-made cabinet as a work of art instead of a good piece of craftsmanship? Is there any danger in it?

Beyond the sloppy use of language (in itself deplorable, but another topic) I would argue that there is, so long as such an association muddies the view of what art really is and what it can do. When everything is art, we no longer see art.

Just as quantum physics had to come around to the realisation that, as viewers, we are inextricable from the results of our observations, so we must concede that in all our affairs we perceive the world through one lens or another. We have gone over the lenses through which Freud viewed people and the mind, the way how the sciences have been a long progression (and at times regression) through the taking on and subsequent abandoning of assumptions about the physical universe, and so too the history of philosophy has shaped the viewpoints of reality and subsequently the cultures of the world through selective filters. Whichever way we carve up our reality, the universe, or our daily lives, is ultimately an illusion; an attempt to make some sense out of the whole chaotic, incessant is-ness of whatever it all is.

But try and make some sense of it we must, unless we wish to live lives no more meaningful than that of a rock. Making incisions with a dialectic knife is fraught with danger. Wherever the diremption is created it can be contested. Contemporary philosopher Jacques Derrida was a specialist in this regard. In his "deconstruction" he sought to pick apart other people's philosophy to show how nothing that anyone said had any meaning, or that it had inherent contradictions derived from the language used to put across their ideas. But this approach is not helpful. Anyone can pull apart anyone else's words if you are of that disposition – it's not big and it's not clever. The whole point of philosophy is to try and make some sense of things, not to try and make a nonsense of everything. There is a place for that, but it is in the field of comedy, not philosophy. Therefore, although the boundaries may all be arbitrary, we have to slice things up somehow, and march headlong into the face of reality with some purpose.

The truths that we have today may be the falsehoods of tomorrow. Several hundred years ago everybody knew the sun revolved around the earth. The concept of gravity may be completely erroneous. Over a century ago, Nikola Tesla provided convincing assertions that the effects attributed to gravity are much more easily and comprehensively explained by electro-magnetic phenomena. And the anomalies suggesting we have something not quite right about gravity are building up in several branches of modern science. We have still managed to achieve a great deal over the last 400 years with the concept outlined by Isaac Newton. Whether it turns out to be completely unfounded, it will remain a huge contribution that served to advance our understanding of the universe. As an aside, Albert Einstein was once asked what it was like to be the cleverest man on the planet. He replied: "I have no idea – you should ask Nikola Tesla".

Summary

In the black and white sides of the yin-yang symbol[22], each contains a part of the other. It could be that nothing in the universe can truly be considered as a separate entity; that all is inherently interconnected and can only be understood by viewing the whole, and that therefore any attempt to define a "not" is fundamentally flawed. Possibly. But that line of reasoning takes us back down the path of "art is everything" and "everything is art", which leads to an unhelpful dead end. We should then have to concede that art is a punch on the nose. Art is a paper bag. The mouldy piece of cheese that you found under the cooker during your spring cleaning, is art. Genocide is art.

I will ask you for the last time to recall your powerful Prime Experience, and ask you this question: would you be happy to live in a world where such an experience had no more meaning or significance than a paper bag? Where it were equated with such an atrocity as genocide? I should think not. In that case, we have to bite the bullet and start to draw up some dividing lines, whether they lead us into difficulty or not. Perhaps they are flexible boundaries, bending to circumstance or drifting over time. As I said in the opening, I don't expect you to whole-heartedly embrace mine, but it behoves you to establish your own.

This is not a futile endeavour. It may be that there is no ultimate answer. We may be staring down the barrel of an unsolvable problem. This doesn't mean we can't duck out of the way and make some forward progress regardless. Consider a familiar example: what colour is a tree? Green. Simple. Except that the trunks and branches are brown, and deciduous trees lose their leaves in winter. So, green and brown. But some trees have purple leaves. Then there is the self-

---

22 More correctly called the *Taijitu,* a symbol from Chinese philosophy, predominantly of the Taoist tradition. It could be said to represent how the seemingly opposite and contradictory forces of nature and the universe are actually interconnected and intertwined, although there are many interpretations of its meaning.

explanatory Redwood and Silver Birch. Spring time brings the pink cherry blossom; Autumn the ambers, golds and finally the yellows. And at night they all turn black.

Suddenly, we find there is no answer that could encompass the myriad of tree colours, apart from the entirely useless and *still* inaccurate answer of "all colours". Our simple question has turned into an unsolvable problem. And yet ask any child what colour a tree is and they will tell you: "it's green". They are usually very uncomplicated about it and they know what they mean.

That there may be exceptions does not prevent us from trying to outline a general truth. The physical sciences are all reliant upon this fact. Anomalies do not stop us from understanding something about the world around us. We can sense where the truths may lie, be they absolute or not. Or, to take on board a more causative viewpoint, an artist is a creator of truths.

As the world moves into the future and technological advances continue to replace the labour of man and provide for his daily necessities, it will become ever more pressing for individuals to engage in alternative pursuits, find and work towards new goals, and develop a new focus for filling the void. An idle man is not a happy one. Wars have been well overdone and are an unsatisfactory pastime for the majority.

Art can certainly fulfil or be a major contributor to this role. But it needs to be cleaned up, the deadwood thrown out, dusted down and polished off before it can be placed, shining upon its throne. If people are to turn to the arts and find degraded pop songs, oceans of shallow YouTube clips with nought but a catchy title, formulaic cookie-cutter blockbusters for which you can tell the ending after the first five minutes, a paint pot thrown at a canvas, then where are they to find their inspiration? Do we not already see the evidences of this being

Summary

played out before us? We have generations of directionless multitudes, idly goggling at the big screens and the small screens and the hand-held screens whilst having the "newest and latest" (regurgitation of the same in different clothes) shovelled down their throats by the truckload. (By the way, art is *not* advertisement. I'll let you figure that one out).

Throughout the nations of Earth there are youthful populations with no real drive, no real purpose, worshipping the false Gods of "fashion" and "celebrity", the mass media and multinational corporations bombarding them with sensory input to tell them what is "cool". It is the minority who see through this to find anything of substance. Such over-exposure serves only to suck power away from these aimlessly meandering individuals, sucking all their attention as it sucks the very life-force out of them. True art is empowering. It restores the vitality, life-force, strength and inspiration to an individual. We need to start separating these things out so we can start to illuminate a path out of the miasma for the wandering souls.

We need to encourage people to take the time and make the effort. Stop flicking through endless channels of rubbish on the TV and seek out the things that give you that deep, heartfelt artistic experience. The positive side to the explosion in global communications and the internet (and it is indeed a very positive side) is that we have instant exposure to a vast array of sources that we never would have come into contact with in days gone by. Artists no longer need contracts, agents, management teams, public relations officers and distribution companies to reach a global market. And what it has shown us is the sheer number of truly brilliant artists and artistic works there are in all corners of the Earth. And it has shown us how many there are in our own home towns, that we can see in the flesh, if we take the trouble to seek them out. It's quite staggering. It's not all about the one or two in the limelight any more. You may have to dig below the surface a little, but we all have spades at our disposal (albeit

193

primarily digital ones these days) and the work is richly rewarded. Hi Ho!

If you are an artist, take the time out to really think about the activity you are engaged in. Make sure you are in touch with yourself and that your focus is in the right place. What are you trying to achieve? Forget about the material considerations for the moment – the "having to take the gig so you can pay the rent", etc. – focus on yourself as an artist. For what are you striving? What made you get into this in the first place? Where are you going with it? Where *should* you be going with it? However you choose to do it, you have to contact that wellspring of creative potentiality, that space between the mental associations, and get it into your work so that others may feed off of it and help to build a new reality. And think about the nature of what you want to create.

Through all of my searching and mental meanderings, I discovered that rather than convince others of what I consider art to be, what I wanted most of all was for other people to think about it. As I said at the outset, I don't expect you to agree with everything I've said. So now it's over to you. What do *YOU* think art is all about?

If I were to provide a simple definition of art, were I able to do such a thing, the response may be "Oh, that's nice", before flicking on the next TV channel. But to think about it oneself is to get into action. It is to evaluate what is important and not important, to come to one's own conclusions, and this, perforce, gives rise to an attitude and state of mind, and engages one on a course. If enough people do this we can build a better world.

Summary

Eleven Things That Art is Not

References

Allan, D.S. & Delair, J.B. (1995) *When the Earth Nearly Died*. Gateway Books (Bath, UK). ISBN: 1 85860 008 1

Aristotle (C.400 BC) *Politics - VIII. VI.*

Atheneus (C.200) *The Deipnosophists; or, Banquet of the Learned of Athenæus*. Translated by C.D. Yonge. EBook #36921, released July 31, 2011 by Project Gutenberg [online] Available at: http://www.gutenberg.org/ebooks/36921 (Accessed 10 May 2018).

Bernstein, J.M. (1992) *The Fate of Art: Artistic Alienation from Kant to Derida and Adorno*. The Pennsylvania State University Press (Pennsylvania). ISBN 0-271-00839-3

Brooks, M. (2008) *Thirteen Things That Don't Make Sense: the most baffling scientific mysteries of our time*. The Doubleday Publishing Group, a division of Random House, Inc. (New York) eISBN: 978-0-385-52673-9

Busoni, F (1907). *Sketch of a New Aesthetic of Music*. Made available by Project Gutenberg [online] Available at http://www.gutenberg.org

Cambridge Dictionary (2018) *Cambridge University press* [online]. Available at: https://dictionary.cambridge.org/us/dictionary/english/art#dataset-american-english (Accessed 7 May 2018)

Dickie, G. (1976) *What is Art* In Lars Aaraarg-Morgensen (ed.), *Culture and Art: An Anthology*. The Humanities Press.

Dictionary.com (2018) *Dictionary.com* [online]. Available at:

http://www.dictionary.com/browse/entertainment (Accessed 6 May 2018)

Ehrmann, M. (1927). *Desiderata*

Frary, P.K. (2017). fraryguitar.com – *Music in the Classical Era, Ludwig van Beethoven* [online] Available at: http://www.fraryguitar.com/history_pages/Classical10.htm (Accessed 6 May 2018)

Freud, Sigmund (1920). *Three Contributions to the Theory of Sex.* Nervous and Mental Disease Publishing Co. Second Edition. (Vienna). Translated by A.A. Brill. PH.B., M.D.

Fricker, G. (2017) *Music is NOT a meritocracy \ SpectreSoundStudios – YouTube.com* [online] Available at: https://www.youtube.com/watch?v=kPVkNVbkIUQ (Accessed 6 July 2018)

Gleick, J. (1987) *Chaos: Making a New Science.* Viking Press

Golding, W. (1959) *Free fall.* Published in 2003 by Mariner Books. ISBN 0156028239

Khan, Sufi Inayat (1959) *Music.* Sufi Publishing Co, Ltd. (Surrey, England). ISBN 0 900217049
King, J. P. (1992) *The Art of Mathematics.* Plenum Press. ISBN 978-0-306-44129-5

Korzybski, A. (1933) *Science and Sanity.* Institute of General Semantics (New York). ISBN 0-937298-01-8.

Mann, J. (2017). Artsy.net – *How Duchamp's Urinal Changed Art Forever* [online]. Available at: https://www.artsy.net/article/artsy

References

-editorial-duchamps-urinal-changed-art-forever (Accessed 6 May 2018)

Merton, R.K. (1961) *Singletons and Multiples in Scientific Discovery: A Chapter in the Sociology of Science*. American Philosophical Society.

Moorcock, Michael (1981). *The Dancers at the End of Time*. Panther Books

Neely, A. (2017) *Q&A #27 Music is NOT a meritocracy – YouTube.com* [online] Available at: https://www.youtube.com/watch?v=3WxPXieXEAQ (Accessed 6 July 2018)

Ogburn, W.F. & Thomas, D. (1922) *Are Inventions Inevitable? A Note on Social Evolution. Political Science Quarterly, Vol.37*. The Academy of Political Science.

Oxford Dictionaries (2018). *English Oxford Living Dictionaries* [online] Available at: https://en.oxforddictionaries.com/definition/entertainment (Accessed 6 May 2018)

Pirsig, R. (1974) *Zen and the Art of Motorcycle Maintenance*. Harper Collins

Plato (C.380 BC) *The Republic*. Oxford University Press (London). Translated by Benjamin Jowett. Ebook #55201 – Released 26 July 2017, made available by *The Gutenburg Project* [online] Available at: http://www.gutenberg.org/ebooks/55201

Poponin, Dr. V. & Gariaev, P. (2002) *The Phantom DNA Effect* [online] Available at: https://www.bibliotecapleyades.net/ciencia/ciencia_genetica04.htm (Accessed 9 July 2018)

Press, B. (2015). *YouTube, page: Squarepusher - Solo Electric Bass, full concert* Available at: https://www.youtube.com/watch?v=gFWjkku2qjQ&t=473s (Accessed 22 March 2018)

Saint-Exupery, Antoine de (1967) *Wind, Sand and Stars.* Harcourt Brace Javanovich (New York). Translated by Lewis Galantiere

Sheldrake, R. (2012) *The Science Delusion.* Coronet (GB) ISBN 978 1 444 72795 1

Songwriters: Alex Zivojinovich / Gary Lee Weinrib / Neil Elwood Peart The Spirit of Radio lyrics © Ole Media Management Lp

Tolkein, J.R.R. (1954) *The Lord of the Rings* Houghton Mifflin Harcourt

Vasari, G. (1550 & 1568) *Lives of the Most Eminent Painters, Sculptors and Architects.* Made available by The Gutenberg Project [online] www.gutenberg.org eBook #25326

Wikipedia (2018) *Wikipedia – Entertainment* [online]. Available at: https://en.wikipedia.org/wiki/Entertainment (Accessed 22 March 2018)

Williamson, M. (1992) *A Return to Love: Reflections on the Principals of "A Course in Miracles".* Available at: https://en.wikiquote.org/wiki/Marianne_Williamson (Accessed 13 April 2019). Text is available under theCreative Commons Attribution-ShareAlike License: https://creativecommons.org/licenses/by-sa/3.0/

Wroth, D. (2015) *Why Songlines are Important in Aboriginal Art* [online]. Available at: https://japingkaaboriginalart.com/articles/songlines-important-aboriginal-art/ (Accessed 28 June 2018)

References

Whistler, J.M. (1890) *The Gentle Art of Making Enemies.* Made available by The Gutenberg Project [online] www.gutenberg.org eBook #24650

Eleven Things That Art is Not

Bibliography

If you are interested in elephants painting, you can start by checking out this link: https://thaielephantart.com

Copyright's Paradox (2008) – Neil Weinstock. Oxford Scholarship ISBN-13: 9780195137620

Day the Universe Changed, The (1985) – James Burke. British Broadcasting Corporation.

Dianetics, The Modern Science of Mental Health (1950) – L. Ron Hubbard. New Era Publications

Fingerprints of the Gods (1995) – Graham Hancock. Phoenix Books

Fundamentals of Thought (1956) – L. Ron Hubbard. New Era Publications

Lucid Dreamer, The (1994) – Malcolm Godwin. Simon and Schuster.

Making of a New World (1973) – John G. Bennet. Harper & Row.

Meditation: An Introduction

Money as Debt – Paul Grignon [online] Available at: https://www.youtube.com/watch?v=2nBPN-MKefA

Music of the Primes, The (2003) Marcus du Sautoy. HarperCollins Publishers, New York. ISBN 0-06-093558-8

Practice of Autosuggestion, The (1911) – Emile Coue

Secret of the Creative Vacuum, The (1989) – John Davidson. C.W. Daniel

Secret Power of Music, The (1984) – David Tame. Inner Traditions/Bear.

Songlines (1987) – Bruce Chatwin. Penguin Group (New York)

Tavistock Institute of Human Relations, The (1991) – Dr. John Coleman

12th Planet, The (1991) – Zecharai Sitchin. Simon and Schuster.

Terrorism and the Illuminati (2011) – David Livingstone. Progressive Press

Tibetan Book Of Living and Dying (2008) – Sogyal Rinpoche. Random House

View Over Atlantis (1972) – John F. Mitchell. Abacus.

www.ingramcontent.com/pod-product-compliance
Lightning Source LLC
Chambersburg PA
CBHW070628220526
45466CB00001B/118